FOR VIDEOS THAT S

THIS BOOK, CHECK OUT...

LEARN TECH COLLECTIVE

www.YouTube.com/LearnTechCollective

JOIN THE LEARN TECH COLLECTIVE FOR FREE RESOURCES

In addition to the Learn Tech Collective YouTube channel, there are even more resources available to those who purchase the book and join the Learn Tech Collective.

TO REGISTER YOUR BOOK, GO HERE:

http://bit.ly/LearnTechCollective

(Case Sensitive URL)

You will receive an email directing you to videos and written

resources that relate to this book. You will also be able to post responses to book activities and ask for advice in a private LinkedIn group. (If you don't have a LinkedIn account, you will need to create one to access this resource.)

You will be able to access all associated resources, for free, for 90 days. If you wish to continue your access after 90 days, you will have the option to pay a small monthly subscription fee. This fee supports the development of new content.

The author and the members of the private LinkedIn group will support you as you learn more about learning technology! This book is offered in print and e-book formats from:

www.Amazon.com

And other retailers

LMS Success!

A Step-by-Step Guide to Learning Management System Administration

Katrina Marie Baker

Resources of Fun Learning
Los Angeles
2018

Published by Resources of Fun Learning

ISBN 978-0-9862469-2-0

A Big Thank You...

I want to thank you, the reader, for being interested in learning technology. This field enables us to teach more people in more places. We are part of something beautiful.

My sincerest appreciation goes to everyone who helped fund my crowdfunding campaign, which helped me republish this book and *The LMS Selection Checklist*. Your names are listed on the Supporters page near the back of the book. It was important to me that I would be able to publish this second edition without giving up control of the content to a publisher. You all allowed me to turn down a major literary contract and follow my heart on the approach to this book.

As with all of my writing, this book is dedicated to my Mom and Dad, and my Grandma. I love you.

Thank you also to Tracie Marie Cantu, my adopted older sis, editor, fellow geek, and feisty cheerleader. And to Kent Russell, for supplying free therapy and a swift kick in the pants.

Finally, love to everyone who says hello on social media or comes up to chat after my sessions. Thank you for telling me your stories.

Contents

INTRODUCTION

WHY, HELLO AGAIN!

Welcome to the second edition of *LMS Success!* This book was originally published in 2014, and it was the first book out there that discussed real-world LMS best practices. It has been an Amazon category bestseller and regularly sells out at learning and development conferences, much to my continued excitement.

This second edition is special because, in addition to the updated written content, this book gives you access to tons of FREE online resources that will help you during your LMS journey. (For details, check out the first pages of this book.) There is a YouTube channel of videos, a selection of documents that save you time, and a private LinkedIn group so that you can post responses to the questions asked in this book. You can also use the group to ask your deepest LMS questions and get help from other administrators!

For many of us, LMS administration is challenging at first. Many people fall into the role, having worked for decades in HR or some area of training that didn't require technical skills. You may have never expected an LMS to figure into your job role, but you will be fine. The role of an LMS administrator is half project management, and half learning and development. You'll learn some technical skills as you go along, but you won't need to become a hard-core programmer or e-learning developer.

The contents of this book are mainly for training managers and brand-new LMS administrators who would like a little reassurance as they wade through the world of learning technology. Everyone is welcome though – instructional designers, our friends in IT, and HR folks may find the content useful. You can read the text straight through or skip to the tips that sound most appealing.

"DO I NEED TO BE A TECHIE TO READ THIS BOOK?"

NO! Before we get started, I'll promise you two things.

- Very little technical knowledge is required. If you can check your email, you are qualified to read this book.
- Everything is written in plain English. If acronyms are used, they're explained. (Do you like nerd-speak? Skip to Chapter 4 for lots of definitions!)

"WHAT CAN I FIND IN THIS BOOK?"

Oh, there's lots of fun stuff!

- Explanations of what an LMS can do for your company
- Suggestions of questions to ask, when to ask them, and what tasks to perform
- Clever ideas that use an LMS to its fullest extent
- Practical advice and anecdotes based on real-life experience
- Lots of activities to help you move through the process of getting to know your system
- Free online resources you can utilize for additional help

As you can tell from the chapter listing, we talk about a variety of important topics:

- Evaluating organizational needs from a learning perspective
- Selecting and implementing an LMS
- Assembling the administrator team
- Training content and course creation resources
- Maintaining the system and handling technical issues
- Realizing the value of your LMS

"YOU MENTIONED RESOURCES; WHERE CAN I FIND THEM?

You deserve to have support as you start your new career path! To receive your supplemental resources, all you need to do is join the Learn Tech Collective. Check out the first pages of this book for instructions.

After registration, you will receive an email with a link to a private LinkedIn group just for readers of this book. This group gives you the ability to post responses to book activities and ask questions of fellow LMS administrators. You will also be directed to "unlisted" YouTube videos that are only visible to members of the private LinkedIn group, and documents that make it easier to complete certain LMS tasks.

"Does this book tell me EVERYTHING about my LMS?"

Nope! This book contains best practices that will help you use any LMS. It will also help you select an LMS, which means you can use the book even before you have a system in place.

Once you select a system, you will want to get lots of information from your LMS vendor. There are HUNDREDS of learning management systems out there, and each one functions a little differently. Throughout the book, we will discuss questions and issues you should address with your vendor.

By the way, if you're currently selecting an LMS, you can check out *The LMS Selection Checklist*, which is available from Amazon and other book retailers.

"Okay, mysterious book writer… who are you?"

Most people call me Kat. I'm known in learning and development for my work as a consultant, speaker, and author. I was an LMS administrator back before that was considered an official job role, and I've selected, implemented, and/or administered nearly thirty platforms. I also enjoy following the latest industry trends and give unbiased advice to whoever asks for it.

The advice in the book has been compiled from my personal experience, along with the experience of LMS administrators who are my friends and mentors.

If there is one thing that sets me apart from other authors and analysts in this industry, it's that I don't participate in corporate referral programs or paid sponsorships. I believe in being totally honest and transparent.

"What the heck is up with that Lightbulb?"

You'll notice two mascots that appear throughout this book:

- Nerdy lightbulb provides resources that will help with the topic at hand
- Nerdy pencil provides you with a homework assignment or question to answer. You can write your answer directly into the book (assuming you have a paperback copy) or post your answer in the private discussion forum

It's great to have you! Before we get started, let's do one formal definition.

What is a learning management system (LMS)?

An LMS is a server or cloud-based software that allows you to plan, implement, and assess learning in many forms. Learning management systems make it possible to deliver training content in many formats, monitor course participation, and assess student performance. A well designed LMS will reduce the amount of time you spend on administrative tasks associated with training. It will also make it easy for learners to find resources and track their progress.

There are many LMS features that help you engage learners, such as gamification, social learning, and web conferencing integrations. A learning management system can be as simple or complex as your company wants it to be.

Besides learning management systems, there are other types of learning technology platforms out there. For example, you may have heard of a Learning Content Management System (LCMS) or Learning Record Store (LRS). If you would like to learn more about these, check out the YouTube channel Learn Tech Collective. View the video *Learning Technology Defined: The Difference Between an LMS, LCMS, and LRS.*

Without further ado, let's talk about how to evaluate your organization's need for a learning management system.

1

Evaluating Your Organization's Needs

What was that quote – it takes a village to raise an LMS? All kidding aside, selecting an LMS requires a team of people, including company leadership. The LMS selection process starts with an exploration of goals. What does your company want to accomplish by implementing an LMS? Your company's goals will define what you look for in a learning management system.

Analyzing Your Company's Needs

As we discussed in the introduction, learning management systems are chock-full of incredible tools that will take your training program to the next level. This doesn't mean you will want or need every LMS feature! Your first challenge will be to determine what your users need from an LMS and translate those needs into a list of system requirements. Look at your training content, and decide how the LMS can best be utilized to support your program.

#1 Determine what your learners need from a learning management system.

Sounds like such an easy question, doesn't it? But in order to determine your learners' needs, you need to know who they are. To get started, consider the following factors that influence what a learner will want from an LMS, and how they will react to it.

- Level of interest in developing new skills
- Prior experience with an LMS and associated content
- Comfort level with technology in general
- Learning medium preferences (Video, e-learning, blended or instructor led?)
- Amount and type of interaction with an LMS (For example, Meagan, a supervisor, accesses content and reviews the learning progress of her team.)

As you think through the learner's characteristics, you begin to build a picture of that learner overall. This broader view of a learner is commonly referred to as a user persona. Researching the user personas within your organization can help you better understand what learners will want to see in your LMS.

Would you like to explore your learners' needs by creating user personas? Additional resources are available in the private LinkedIn group. Flip to the front of the book for details.

#2 Before you begin searching for the right LMS, speak with your company's executive leadership. What are their goals for the LMS?

Once you've built an understanding of your learners, you need to get an idea of how leadership feels about your current LMS, if you have one, and what they want to see from a new LMS. You will want to speak with leadership from all departments or groups within your organization. Use the questions below to start off your discussion or guide it in different directions.

Additional resources are available in the private LinkedIn group.

- Which departments or groups within your organization will use the LMS, and in what ways? Do they have specific goals to accomplish using the new LMS?
- If your organization currently has an LMS, how do these departments or groups utilize it?
- How many people will be system administrators? Just a few, or will you have a representative from every department?
- What types of content will you deliver through the LMS? Interactive games, documents, videos, exams?
- Will you use the system to deliver content that is proprietary or sensitive? Do you have security concerns that should be discussed with the LMS vendors you are considering?
- Will you use the system to deliver compliance courses?
- Will you track content that lives outside of the LMS? For instance, you might want to track articles a learner reads on the Internet or classes a learner is taking at a local university.
- Using the LMS, will your company provide training content to all levels of employees? Just leadership? Will you provide content to external parties, such as customers?
- Think of ALL of the training currently performed by your company. How many of your classes could be delivered through the learning management system? How much

do you want to continue relying on instructor-led classes?

- Will the platform be made available in one language, or will the user be able to choose from several languages?
- Do you need the system to deliver specific reports regarding employee course completion?
- What features will drive engagement? For instance, you might want a mobile-friendly LMS or a system that allows users to compete against each other, or interact using discussion boards. (You can Google "social learning" or "gamification LMS" for more information.)

#3 After discussing the above points, begin forming goals for your LMS.

Not all learning management systems are alike! Each LMS vendor offers a different system with unique tools and features. Since each system has strengths and weaknesses, preparing a list of goals for your LMS will help you evaluate what features will be most helpful.

Write down at least three specific goals that your executive leadership has for your learning management system. If desired, share these goals and solicit feedback from others in the LinkedIn group.

#4 Translate your LMS goals, user personas, and organizational feedback into a requirements list for the new LMS. You will refine this over time.

As you collect information, feedback, and more from your organization, ask yourself what features you will want or need in your new learning management system. It's fine to write down features and items you don't think you can afford. It's also fine to write down things that only some groups in your organization will want or need.

Once you've written down all of your desired LMS features, prioritize them. You can do this in many ways, but I personally recommend creating an Excel spreadsheet of requirements and sending it to your stakeholders so they can rank the items in order of importance. Compile the rankings, and you'll know which features you'll want to inquire about when speaking with LMS vendors.

Need a list of LMS features to use as a starting point for your list? Check out ***The LMS Selection Checklist***, available on Amazon.

Would you like a template to use when prioritizing your LMS requirements? One is provided to you when you join the LinkedIn group! You can begin filling out the template now and continue adding to it as you read through Chapter 1. Details can be found in the front of the book.

#5 If you begin delivering the majority of your company's training through an LMS, how much could your company save on expenses?

How much does it cost your company to offer a "classroom training," also known as an ILT (Instructor-Led Training)? Researching the cost of these classes will allow you to better evaluate how much you can spend on a new LMS because you'll know how much money it will save you.

Use the following forms to guide your cost research. Consider the expense of instructors, the labor involved in a classroom set-up, the cost of meals, travel, and room rentals, etc.

Once you have an estimated total of the average expense per class, you can divide this figure by your average number of class attendees. (Use the second table.) This will tell you how much it costs, per employee, to deliver a classroom training. Provide this number to your executive leadership when it is time to evaluate the cost of learning management systems and the associated e-learning content. It's a great benchmark!

Estimated Costs of an Instructor-Led Training	
Listed below are some expenses associated with classroom training. Consider a typical training conducted by your company. In the right-hand column, list the amount you spend on each cost category.	
Cost of Instructor's Time in Classroom	
Cost of Instructor's Time Registering Attendees	
Cost of Attendees' Time	
Training Materials	
Classroom Rental	
Equipment Rental	
Meals Provided to Attendees	
Travel Costs (Mileage, Hotel, Rental Cars)	
Other	
Total Cost	

Average Number of Attendees	
Total Cost/Number of Attendees	

Below, brainstorm some guidelines you can use to determine whether a specific training should remain an instructor-led training, or be converted to a computer-based ("e-learning") training. For instance, would you like all training for new hires to be done in person so instructors can establish a personal connection? Would you like to move all safety courses to your LMS so you can easily assign them to your entire employee base?

If desired, share your thoughts in the LinkedIn group.

#6 How many individuals will use the LMS? What is your projected growth?

The number of users accessing your LMS will affect how much your company spends to maintain the system. Many LMS vendors charge a flat, annual rate to use their software – plus a per-user rate – over the course of a three-year contract. Per-user rates vary by vendor. Generally, the more users you have, the less your company will pay per user.

Jot down how many employees you currently have in your company, as well as an estimate of your company's growth in coming years. (If you think that you may want to give LMS access to your leadership group only, **skip to tip #10** and come back after completing that activity.)

Current Employee Count	
# of Employees One Year from Now	
# of Employees Three Years from Now	

Armed with these figures, ask the vendors you consider to give you an estimate of annual costs for their system. (If you have not yet identified potential vendors, you can skip forward in this chapter to the **"Selecting a Vendor"** section.) Be sure they include their per-user cost, if applicable. It is important to ask LMS vendors for a rough estimate of costs early in your selection process.

Plug estimated costs into the following table to determine approximately how much you will spend on your system during the first year. If your employee count will increase significantly in coming years, keep in mind that your system cost may increase as well. Be sure the projected budget for your system allows for the growth of your employee base.

LMS Vendor #1: ___________________________	
Cost Charged Per User	
Cost x Current Employee Count	
Flat Annual Service Charges	
Total Estimated Costs	

LMS Vendor #2: ___________________________	
Cost Charged Per User	
Cost x Current Employee Count	
Flat Annual Service Charges	
Total Estimated Costs	

LMS Vendor #3: ___________________________	
Cost Charged Per User	
Cost x Current Employee Count	
Flat Annual Service Charges	
Total Estimated Costs	

#7 Know your budget - not just now, but for the future.

Oh, these vendors and their fees! As we have discussed, your LMS vendor may charge your company an annual flat fee, plus a fee per user. Be sure you ask potential LMS vendors for their estimated costs. That sparkly new system with all of the bells and whistles may not be a good match for your budget!

Assuming you ask potential LMS vendors for estimates and their rate is reasonable - is your rate locked in? For how long? Get this in writing. A word of caution...

It is not uncommon for LMS vendors to raise the cost of their software when it is time to renew your company's contract. I know a lot of LMS administrators, and some of them have horror stories regarding contract renewals. For instance, there is a large corporation that invested a great deal of time and effort into adopting an LMS. A year after implementation, the company's vendor **more than**

doubled their annual per-user cost. Seriously! The company ended up investing hundreds of thousands more per year than they had initially budgeted for their LMS. Don't let this happen to you! Ask your LMS vendor for references, and ask their current customers if they have seen major cost increases.

Check out YouTube channel Learn Tech Collective for more tips on negotiating your LMS contract.

Let's take a look at how your company's annual LMS budget compares to the costs associated with your potential vendors.

Your Company's Annual LMS Budget	
What is your company's annual budget for the learning management system? How does your allotted budget compare to the estimated annual costs of the LMS vendors you researched in #4?	
Annual Costs: Vendor #1	
Annual Costs: Vendor #2	
Annual Costs: Vendor #3	

Your Company's Annual Budget	
Which LMS Vendors Match Your Budget?	

Important! Remember you can, and should, negotiate the price! Before selecting your LMS, please complete the rest of the activities in this section. They will help you evaluate the features of various systems, so you choose the LMS that best suits all of your company's needs. They will also give you handy discussion points to use when speaking with vendors.

Write down some important points to discuss with LMS vendors in order to determine whether their system is a good match for your objectives. Taking into consideration your discussions and research up to this point, what are your company's main goals for the LMS? How important will the system be to your company's training culture? Do you have any specific concerns an LMS vendor will need to address early on?

Remember, you can continue adding to your LMS requirements template as you read through this chapter. Once you are finished, you can provide the document to prospective vendors so they can tell you how their LMS stacks up. If you have questions, you can ask in the LinkedIn group.

#8 How many system administrators will you need to support your LMS?

Discuss with company leadership whether there will be a budget for LMS administrators. Here are some potential discussion questions:

- How many people can your company devote to administering your LMS?
- Do you have employees who are technically capable of being an LMS administrator and/or e-learning developer?
- Are those same employees capable of handling your LMS without having a minor psychotic episode or destroying vital company equipment? (Some people are just not cut out for IT work.)

You might be saying, "Wait a minute. How would I know? I'm not even sure what an LMS administrator does." (It's all good; we will address all of that in a later section of this book.)

You can nail down specifics later, but during these early planning stages, you do want to consider whether you have employees who can function as system administrators.

If you have employees who are capable of functioning as system administrators, will these people be full-time admins, or will they perform other functions outside of the LMS? Many companies have trainers who serve as LMS administrators while fulfilling other responsibilities. When I started out as an LMS admin, being a system administrator was one small aspect of my job as a corporate trainer.

If your company can't afford a full-time system administrator, do you want to outsource certain tasks associated with the system? Some LMS vendors provide such services to their customers.

Begin reflecting on who in your company may be able to help with LMS administration and/or content creation for your system. Jot down any names below. We will discuss system administration in detail later in this book.

#9 Do you want employees to access e-learning content from home, or only on the company network?

Essentially, this boils down to whether or not you want employees to be able to access training content at home on their own time. Your immediate reaction may be a resounding yes, but there are legal implications.

Let's say you have two employees competing for a promotion. One employee has been taking courses on your LMS from home – the other hasn't. The latter employee could accuse your company of favoring the first employee based solely on their completion of e-learning courses. (Yes, it really has happened!) In other words, making your LMS available from any computer on the Internet could have unintended legal issues.

For this reason, you may want to ask your LMS vendor whether it is possible to make your learning management system available only through your company intranet, assuming you have one. Explore this issue with your company's leadership early in the LMS selection process, so that you can discuss your needs with your LMS vendor.

Another option is to post a statement on the LMS home page stating that employees should only use the learning management system on paid company time if that is indeed the case.

So, will your employees be able to access content from home or only on the company network? Jot down your decision and reasons.

#10 Will all of your employees have access to the LMS?

This is an important question to address early in your LMS selection process. If all of your employees will have access to your learning management system, your number of users will be significantly higher. This is good and bad. Giving all employees LMS access will obviously increase the impact of your online courses and give you a greater return on your system. All kinds of learning possibilities open up!

You will be able to offer a variety of compliance and company culture courses to new hires; you can deliver safety and compliance documents and courses; and the training data you deliver to leadership will be much more impressive, hopefully leading to more financial support for the LMS.

There are only two downsides to making your LMS available to all employees company-wide. First, there is the issue of expense (discussed earlier in this section). Many LMS vendors will charge you a flat annual fee, plus a fee per user. The higher your number of users, the higher the total expense of your LMS will be.

Second, you will have more users who need to learn how to use the LMS. It follows that you will probably need more admins to answer user questions. Plus, you will have more employees who need technical support, more people who may need courses designed in different languages or with heightened accessibility features, and you will have more people asking for a broader range of course topics. None of these things are bad – they're just factors you should keep in the back of your mind.

Catering to the needs of your entire employee base will be challenging, especially during the LMS roll-out phase. However, the end result will be rewarding, both for employees and for your company as a whole.

Choose your poison: Will all of your employees have access to the LMS?

YES **NO**

#11 How will your LMS integrate with, or link to, existing company systems?

When you are shopping for your learning management system, you will notice that many vendors offer other management systems designed to work with their LMS.

Here is an example: Some vendors offer an applicant tracking system. (An ATS is essentially a job site, where open positions are listed for recruiting purposes.) An employee can log onto one dashboard and easily access information relating to both the LMS and the applicant tracking system.

Depending on your company's needs, you may want to purchase an all-inclusive software package that incorporates human resource management software, a learning management system, and other systems under one "umbrella." If your company purchases multiple systems from the same vendor, the combined cost is sometimes lower, and it may be easier to manage the system integrations.

For example, let's say you purchase a human resource information system along with your LMS and then integrate the two. The HRIS can tell the LMS software when a new employee has been added to the company roster. The LMS software can then create log-on credentials for the employee and instantly assign the courses you have specified for new hires. How nifty is that?

As you start talking to LMS vendors, get their ideas regarding ways to integrate the LMS with other systems.

Below, write down other software packages and/or features that may help your company in the future. These could include an applicant tracking system (ATS) or human resource information systems (HRIS aka ERP) software and the like. Feel free to post in the LinkedIn group and ask for additional ideas. Include this information in the requirements list that you have been creating throughout this chapter.

#12

Do all of your employees have email addresses?

Some companies only provide email addresses to members of leadership. Limiting the number of company email addresses cuts down on the amount of server space need for email storage. It also decreases the number of users requesting technical support. ("*My Outlook just crashed for the fifteenth time today!!!*")

Just for the record, circle the appropriate answer below: Do all employees have email addresses?

YES **NO**

You can run most learning management systems regardless of whether all employees have a company email address. However, if all of your LMS users have a company email address, many administrative tasks become easier. A few basic examples follow.

- Each time you hire a new employee, your LMS could automatically send the employee an email with their log-on information.

- Let's say an employee has used the LMS to register for instructor-led training. If you make changes to the time or date of the class, your LMS can send attendees the updated information in an email.
- If an employee has overdue courses, the LMS can send them an email reminder.
- Let's say you need to reset passwords for a large group of employees. Most learning management systems will allow you to reset the group's passwords with one touch of a button, and the system will send password reset emails to all affected employees.

Keep in mind that some learning management systems aren't able to perform some of the above functions. If there is a specific function you definitely want, be sure to add it to your requirements list.

#13 What will your employees use as their LMS username?

When using your learning management system, each of your employees will access their account by entering a username and password. Depending on your system, employees may also enter a "company ID" so the LMS knows which company's profile the employee is attempting to access.

If your company issues employee identification numbers or the like, you may want to set this number as the LMS username for all of your employees. That way, each employee automatically knows their username. If your human resource management system connects to your learning management system, it should be easy to import all employee ID numbers into your LMS. Mention this to your LMS vendor – see how they think you should handle issuing usernames for your employees.

When your LMS is first implemented, all employees will be issued a temporary password (often the same as their username). In other words, an employee (with Employee ID 999) accessing your LMS for the first time may enter the following:

Company ID: <your company name>
Username: 999
Password: 999

Employees will be prompted to reset their temporary password to one of their choosing when they log onto the LMS for the first time. Ask your LMS vendor what will happen if an employee forgets their password. Many learning management systems allow users to set security questions that they can answer in order to reset their passwords. Other systems may require that passwords be manually reset by a system administrator. Depending on the size of your company, manual password resets may significantly add to the workload of your LMS administrators. We will discuss administrator tasks more in a later section of this book.

What information will your employees use as their LMS username? (Examples: Employee ID number, firstname.lastname, etc.)

What procedure will be used to reset passwords?

2

Selecting & Implementing a Learning Management System

Selecting an LMS vendor is like picking a spouse. (Okay, I'm exaggerating a little...) You will be in regular contact with your vendor throughout the implementation, and your company will rely on their advice, technical support, and training for years. The relationship with your vendor can make or break your LMS.

Selecting a Vendor

There are several hundred LMS vendors on the market, which is why it's so important to know what your users want before you start evaluating vendors. Anticipate looking at fifteen or twenty vendors. You'll get into detailed discussions with several of them, and eventually narrow to two or three top contenders. This section will guide you through that process.

#1 Know what you want and know your priorities.

If you've been reading Chapter 1, you've likely put together a requirements list for your new LMS. (You may have used the free template available to members of the LinkedIn group.)

That's a perfect start. Also, make sure to assign priorities to your requirements. For instance, your organization may consider having a mobile-friendly LMS an absolute necessity. You might consider social learning features to be less critical, but still a factor for consideration. As you create your requirements list, note next to each item what the priority is. If you've been using Learn Tech Collective's requirements template, note that it includes fields that help you prioritize requirements and score vendors.

For instance, you might create a spreadsheet like this:

Mobile friendly LMS	Required
Discussion forums for online courses	Important but not critical
The ability for users to rank completed courses from one to five stars	Entirely optional

(When you share your requirements list with vendors, don't include the priorities!)

At the end of the day, no LMS is going to be a perfect match. The important thing is to find an LMS that fulfills everything you need, and most of what you want, for an amount you can afford.

Once your requirements list is ready, begin researching LMS vendors, and share some of your biggest priorities with several of them. If a vendor seems like a good match, send them your full requirements list and have them comment on what features they're able to provide. (Make sure your list is a reasonable length, around 30-40 items at maximum.) Ultimately, you will end up with a side by side comparison of a few vendors, and you can then ask them to provide targeted demos for your organization.

#2 Research learning management system options and do your best to avoid biased information.

You may have seen posts about different learning management systems on social media. There are plenty of articles about how such-and-such LMS was "chosen as the #1 LMS" in gamification, social learning, blended learning, you name it.

The best learning technology is whatever suits the needs of your organization. And every organization is different.

There are tons of LMS comparison reports on the Internet, and there's a reason. The people creating them get paid by learning technology vendors who want a shiny badge to put on their platform. A gold star to make them stand out amongst hundreds of other vendors.

I'm not saying they are doing something wrong. If I'd created a product, and my livelihood was based on sales, certainly I'd be motivated to find creative ways to market my goods.

So vendors buy spots on LMS comparison reports. They pay to be considered and ranked. Independent LMS consultants are paid a lot of money to provide sound bites, endorsements, and white papers saying how stupendous a particular LMS is.

Since I began selling my LMS books, I've been offered payment, kickbacks, and all sorts of other deals to endorse products, or refer clients to a particular vendor. I've never accepted payment from a vendor for any of these things. But there are plenty of people who do.

(As a quick aside, I have no problem with any consultant who partners with a vendor and is upfront about it. I just think it's important to be honest about affiliations. If someone is paying you, say so.)

Here are some tips to help avoid biased sources of information while selecting your learning management system:

- Rather than relying on industry analysts, go to your colleagues who use a learning management system. Ask other companies what LMS vendor they use and if they like them.

- Attend a conference with a big vendor expo, like ATD International. Talk to lots of people and see what vendor names keep popping up.
- Ask LMS vendors for client references. Call the references. (See #4 in the following pages.) And look on LinkedIn ahead of time to make sure the references are real people. (I once asked a vendor for client references, and to my surprise, I actually had one of the phone numbers he gave me in my phone contacts list. The phone number belonged to a developer *who worked for the vendor*. Hmm!)
- If an LMS vendor won't give you client names and instead offers you a client testimonial video, that's not the same thing. Keep asking for their references.
- If you decide to hire an independent LMS consultant to select your LMS, ask if they've ever been affiliated with a vendor. Then look at their social media to see if they've given you an honest answer. It's okay for a consultant to have worked with a vendor. The question here is whether the consultant is willing to be honest about their affiliation.
- Before you hire an independent consultant, Google them and see what comes up. If a consultant is spending a lot of time and effort promoting a specific LMS platform, there's a good chance that vendor is paying them. You can still take the consultant's advice. Just understand where they are coming from.

Here is a quick reference list of factors you should look for in a vendor. When you are speaking to someone about their LMS, see whether they are satisfied with the below:

- Timely customer service
- Knowledgeable technical support
- Number of technical support representatives
- Willingness to customize the system and make changes as needed
- Creative company mindset and a desire to innovate
- Minimal system downtime and a lack of major technical issues
- How long the company has been in business
- Size of customer base
- Financial stability
- Respectable company reputation
- Security features and regular data back-ups
- Ability to easily import data from another LMS
- Software features or integrations that support your company's objectives

As you research different vendors, feel free to share your findings with our LinkedIn group and ask others which vendors they are learning about.

#3 Is the LMS vendor successful?

Implementing an LMS requires a lot of hard work! Ideally, you do not want to implement another LMS for a few years or more. Is the LMS vendor financially stable? Are they respected within the learning and development industry? Is this vendor accustomed to working with companies of similar size to yours? Is the company offering any other software or services that would potentially support your company's growth in the future?

Check out potential LMS vendors by searching the Internet and looking around on LinkedIn. Can you find any news articles that suggest the vendors are working on new innovations, are financially stable, or are respected within the training industry? Write down your findings below, or share in the LinkedIn group.

#4 What kind of customer service experience can you expect?

You are about to start a long-term relationship with your LMS vendor's Customer Service department. Talk to other companies who currently use the vendor's products. Do they respond to requests quickly? Are there frequent technical issues and downtime? Your LMS should work for you, not the other way around!

Contact at least two companies currently using the services of each vendor you are seriously considering. Write down each company's feedback about the vendors below. If you feel comfortable, share your research with the LinkedIn group.

Ask about each system's reliability, the amount of downtime, the number of glitches, and whether users have had an easy time adapting to the system's interface. Ask if the LMS vendor has been responsive to technical support requests. If you can speak with companies that are the same approximate size as your company, that is ideal.

#5 Which vendors offer the features your company needs? Schedule demos with your top contenders.

Once you have done some research on your LMS options, you will, of course, want to circle back to each vendor. Ask questions about any negative insights provided by their references. Review with the vendor your objectives, and explore how their LMS can help your company achieve its goals. The more specific you can be, the better. Is the LMS vendor willing and able to customize your system to the extent you will need? Can they show you examples of user interfaces they have designed, so you can gather ideas?

As mentioned earlier, it's a good idea to share your requirements list with a few vendors that are serious contenders. It's also wise to set up demos so that you can see their LMS in action. If you can get a free trial so you can explore the platform yourself, that's even better.

Based on the activities completed earlier in this book, write down at least three features or functions you would like to explore during a vendor demo. The vendor will definitely take you on a tour of the user interface, but maybe you also want to see the administrator interface, the reporting capabilities, and the learning paths.

The vendor demo should help you evaluate each vendor's ability to fulfill your company's needs and further your training objectives. Remember to ask about the cost of each system. Bring your questions to initial talks with LMS vendors.

#6 How long will it take to build your system and make it available to employees?

At this point, you probably have one or two vendors who stand out amongst the rest. Follow-up questions for each vendor are presented in the remainder of this section. Asking these questions will hopefully help you make your final choice.

Ask your vendor how long it will take to implement your LMS. This time frame will vary greatly depending on the amount of customization you are requesting. Many vendors offer a standard implementation timeline of 90 days, and some offer an expedited timeline for an additional charge.

If you are currently using an LMS, there will be a process to convert the data from your old LMS into a format that can be imported into your new system. This import process can be simple or complex depending on the compatibility between your old and new systems.

The information transferring from your old system to your new system will include training data, and potentially employee information. The import of training data will include information about the courses that existed in your old system, as well as employee transcripts.

Ask your LMS vendor exactly what information will be imported, especially if your old system was involved in the delivery of compliance courses. You will want to be sure the records of those past courses are fully accessible in case you need them for legal purposes.

In order to create accounts for your LMS users, various employment information may be imported (hire date, department, job code, company location, etc.) Employment information can be imported into an LMS in a variety of ways. If your LMS has the capability of hooking into your human resource information system, the two systems can be integrated so that employment information will flow into your LMS from the HRIS. Tell your LMS vendor what HRIS you have, and let them tell you what the import process looks like. Be sure to loop in the appropriate members of IT from your organization.

The employment information stored in your LMS will prove useful when you begin assigning training aimed at specific segments of employees. For example, let's say a particular compliance training must be completed on an employee's hire date. This training must be redone every two years following the employee's hire date. If your employees' hire dates are imported into the LMS, you can program most systems to automatically reassign the compliance training, on the correct date, every two years to **every single employee**! Talk about a major time-saver!

If applicable, tell your LMS vendor which learning management system your company has been using. Have the vendor run a "trial import" of data from your old system to your new system to see if everything works properly.

As you begin getting into discussions of system integrations and data imports, remember that you have resources around you. Your IT department and LMS vendor can and should explain the technical processes associated with your implementation. Every organization has a different situation. Some are simple, and some not so much. Asking for help is always a good idea. Reach out via the LinkedIn group if you want a hand.

How long does your LMS vendor believe it will take to implement your system? Enter their estimate below. If possible, get the anticipated timeframe in writing!

#7 Will you deliver sensitive content through the LMS? What security features can you implement?

If your LMS delivers training content that contains sensitive information, you may want to consider whether you want the LMS to be available to employees from home. In other words, you may want to have your LMS live on your company network (or intranet) rather than on the Internet. This point is discussed earlier in this book, but it is worth revisiting with your vendor before you make final decisions on system implementation. Also, ask what other security measures your vendor can implement for extra protection.

How would implementing these security features affect the amount of time needed to implement your system?

If it takes extra time and effort to address your security needs, don't be discouraged! The end result is worth it. Sure, an LMS is mainly intended to deliver training content, but with the right security, you can use your system to deliver and store HR paperwork electronically. Once your LMS is implemented, you can upload your company's employment documents to the system and assign them to individuals or groups of employees as needed. Most learning management systems allow users to electronically sign documents, which may eliminate a lot of unnecessary paperwork floating around your corporate office. Bet you didn't know your LMS was an office organizer, did you?

Before we get too enamored with the concept of electronic documents, be sure to consult your attorney to rule out any legal issues. You can't be too careful.

#8 Are you going to maintain the LMS on your own server, or use the LMS vendor's server?

Determine the pros and cons of each method. Circle your decision below.

Company Server   **LMS Vendor's Server**

Some LMS vendors require that you use their server because they only offer a cloud-based solution. This is becoming more and more common in the learning technology industry.

Up until recently, many organizations resisted using cloud-based technology due to security and data privacy concerns. But storing data *anywhere* is a risk. Your company can be hacked, as can your vendor. You just have to evaluate which option is the better choice for your situation. It's important to ask your vendor how they will safeguard your data, and certainly, your Security department should be looped in to ask questions.

If your company has locations in other countries, ask your organization's legal counsel whether there are any special considerations as to how data generated in those countries is stored. Some data may need to be stored within the country where it was generated. There may also be data your organization is not legally allowed to collect or store.

There may be a cost associated with the server space provided to you for storage of training content. Ask your vendor for their policy and associated costs. Also, ask where your provider's servers are located. It's always helpful when your vendor has servers and backup servers in two separate locations. If a natural disaster occurs near one set of servers, your company's data will still be safe on the other set of servers.

#9 Do you have data back-ups in place?

Your learning management system will store a great deal of information about employees. It may also store information about compliance training that your company needs for legal purposes.

Ask your LMS vendor what type of data back-ups they offer. How often will the back-ups take place? How easy will it be to restore data in the event of a system failure or natural disaster?

LMS Interface & Associated Tasks

Do a thorough walk-through of the tools and interfaces in your chosen LMS. Does everything work as you would expect? The more creative your vendor is, the more likely they will be to work with you on modifying your system and creating custom tools and interfaces. The more customized your system is, the less time you will spend convincing it to do your bidding.

#1 Take a look at the employee home page. Can it be used to market training programs and classes?

There are lots of ways you can spruce up the employee home page of your LMS! (This is where employees land right after they log onto the system. The page usually includes information about assigned tasks and classes, but you can add more information if you would like.) The home page is prime real estate – use it to market your training program!

Here are some ways to use the employee home page:

- If your training department has a logo, put it on there! There's no better place!
- Insert a flow chart showing different career paths in your company. Include links to classes related to each career path.
- If your LMS has gamification features, include a leaderboard on the home page that displays which individuals or teams in your company have participated.
- If your LMS allows users to rank courses, ask your vendor if you can feature a "top ten" of the most popular courses.
- You may want to have a place on the home page where your employees can view upcoming instructor-led classes available at their location.
- Create a Twitter feed for your company's training program! Embed the feed in the employee homepage so employees see the latest news from your training team.
- Does your company offer tuition reimbursement or college scholarships? Advertise these benefits multiple times a year, around the time employees would be registering for college classes.
- Place a link on the home page that leads to a document explaining common LMS technical issues and their solutions.
- When you first introduce the LMS, embed a short welcome video into the home page to provide users with a quick system tour.

- Embed videos of your company leadership discussing pertinent company issues.

The possibilities for your employee home page are endless! Just be sure to keep the content updated, and advertise only a few items at a time. The LMS home page should be clean, well-designed, and appealing to your employees.

Jot down some ideas for your LMS employee home page. Share your ideas with the LinkedIn group if desired, and ask others for their ideas.

#2 Have your LMS vendor walk you through a few learning sessions from an average user's perspective.

How tech-savvy is your average employee? During these demos, do your best to view the LMS through the eyes of one of your employees. What areas are confusing? How can you address these challenges?

Evaluate the following points during the walk-through.

- How complicated is the log-on process?
- Is the home page self-explanatory and user-friendly for the computer-challenged?
- How easy is it to search for and launch courses?
- Take a course in every format available. In other words, watch a training video, play an interactive game, launch an electronic document, try a multi-module course, etc.
- If your employees will use the system to register for instructor-led classes, how easy is the registration process?
- Take an assessment. Does the procedure make sense? Is it easy to answer questions?
- Can an average user run a "transcript" of their completed courses?
- Ask your vendor to show you any tools specifically intended for a manager or supervisor. How friendly are these tools? Will using these tools cause supervisors to hate the system? Annoyed supervisors will grumble to employees and turn them against the LMS. This we do not want!
- Take a very thorough tour of the administrator dashboard, commonly known as the system's back-of-house. Really concentrate. Squint. Does the dashboard confuse you? How bad is the headache? Your admins are going to spend a lot of time back there. Make sure the dashboard makes sense.

#3 Ask your LMS vendor: What regular tasks would they recommend for your administrators?

We will discuss the role of your administrators in a later section, but for now, ask your vendor what administrator tasks will be necessary to maintain the system. This is an ideal discussion to have while you are doing the walk-through of the administrator dashboard. Will your admins be responsible for uploading course content, or is that the responsibility of the LMS vendor? What about the system implementation process? Will administrators play a role in formatting or uploading data during the implementation? (Have your LMS vendor handle this if at all possible. Uploads can be very time-consuming.)

Note your vendor's answers below. Get any promises of support in writing.

#4 If you are offering courses that will have multiple modules or sections, ask your LMS vendor to show you an example of a multi-module course.

You have likely seen a multi-module course before. They typically start with a table of contents within the LMS interface that lists multiple modules. Once you click on and complete the first module, you are brought back to the table of contents where you click on and complete the next module. (This procedure may be slightly different depending on the system.) Multi-module courses are quite spiffy because they allow you to blend videos, games, written content, and more into one course. They can include multiple assessments and a variety of training content. Splitting up a long course into multiple modules allows your employees to quit the course after completing a module, and come back to complete the next module when they have time.

As a note, if your LMS vendor doesn't offer this sort of course delivery option, you can also build multi-module courses using e-learning development software. Being able to do this within an LMS just saves a bit of course development time.

It is important that the navigation for multi-module courses be clear and easy to understand. Have your LMS vendor show you such a course. With the average user be able to navigate without a lot of instruction? What modifications would make navigation easier?

ASSEMBLING A PLAN FOR IMPLEMENTATION

Quite a few of us hear the words "learning management system implementation" and run for the hills. It's natural to be afraid of taking on a project that is outside of your normal, everyday function.

#1 Be confident in the fact that you can select and implement your own learning management system.

I often speak at conferences about how to best implement an LMS. Sounds exciting, doesn't it? For some reason, not everyone gets as enthusiastic as I do when talking about system integrations and course assignments.

After one of my recent presentations, one of the attendees came up to me and said, "I just want you to tell me it's going to be okay." It can be scary when you're faced with a technology implementation, especially when it's not part of your usual role.

With that in mind, here are some myths and truths I've frequently heard, from clients and other learning professionals.

MYTH: "There's no way I can lead my company's LMS implementation."

I've done tons of LMS selections and implementations. They can be complex, but they aren't rocket science. Rolling an LMS is just a big project. You need good project management skills, a willingness to learn new technical skills, and, most importantly, time.

The most critical part of any LMS implementation is your project plan. Make sure you have a basic understanding of LMS administration. Break your implementation into individual tasks, and assign timelines and responsible parties. (Check out the LinkedIn group resources for help with this!) Work closely with your LMS vendor. They often provide at least a partial timeline you can use as a starting point.

MYTH: "I have to find a consultant who can run my LMS implementation!"

You don't need a consultant to run your implementation. It's entirely your choice. An ironic statement coming from your author, who has been a consultant on a pretty regular basis!

TRUTH: There are times you may want an LMS consultant.

You need one when a) you don't have the time to take on the project yourself, or b) you don't have a desire to work through some of the technical topics required to complete all of the tasks. Don't hire a consultant because you feel like you can't do it. You can and you will!

#2 Determine a project plan for your implementation.

The most critical part of any LMS implementation is your project plan. Break your implementation into individual tasks, and assign timelines and responsible parties. If you've never done this before, ask your LMS vendor for help. They can provide at least a partial timeline you can use as a starting point.

Some tasks are going to be more complex than others. If you feel overwhelmed when you think about any specific task, divide it into smaller tasks that are easier to accomplish.

You can also group tasks by dividing your implementation into five phases, like this:

1: Before a vendor is selected
2: After a vendor is selected
3: During contract negotiations
4: Before go-live
5: After go-live

In the following pages, I've listed some individual LMS implementation tasks you may want to figure into your timeline. A sample implementation plan is available if you are a member of the LinkedIn group. If you prefer to create your own plan, you can create a list of your implementation tasks in Excel or Project, and assign start and end dates for each task. Remember to assign a responsible person for each task. If you would like individualized help putting together your implementation plan, feel free to post in the LinkedIn group.

I've participated in nearly thirty LMS implementations, and the list of tasks has been different for each. I add and delete, and the timeline is always different. Know that the plan you create is a starting point – not a prescribed plan. Also, note that some of these tasks do not directly pertain to the LMS. Many organizations take their LMS implementation as an opportunity to restructure their training department, so you'll see some of those elements as well.

#3 Consider how you should prepare in order to assign critical and compliance courses in the new LMS. Here are some possible tasks to get you started.

- Create a list of compliance courses required of all personnel.

- Create a list of compliance courses required for specific regions or countries.
- Create a list of compliance courses required for specific personnel.
- For all compliance courses - is completion required one time or on a recurring basis?
- Standardize classes provided to new hires.
- Create a list reflecting courses, personnel to receive them, and whether courses should be automatically assigned based on a set of rules (assuming your LMS can perform auto assignments.)
- Do you want a standard group of courses to be pushed to personnel on their hire date? Or three months after they've joined? Or every year during their employment?
- Should compliance courses be maintained in paper formats as an alternative, in case of a system failure?

#4 Consider what tasks will enable you to assemble the LMS course catalog. Should some of these questions and activities be included in the LMS implementation plan?

- Are there any courses in your current LMS that should not be transferred to the new LMS?
- Determine names for all course categories and subcategories.

- Compare existing courses and determine which are similar enough to be merged when you migrate to the new LMS. (Many organizations have duplicate courses because administrators sometimes forget to check whether a course has already been added.)
- Mark corporate events and other non-training courses in the course catalog spreadsheet so they can be categorized appropriately and/or eliminated. (A lot of organizations use their LMS as an event management system. This can really clutter your course catalog.)
- Correct categories, subcategories, delivery, and course unit types for all courses, on a spreadsheet.
- Determine course catalog import structure. (Ask your new LMS vendor about this. It's different for every system.)
- Should courses in all languages be displayed in the same catalog? In multiple catalogs?
- Assign college levels (100 level, 200 level, and so on) so curricula are assigned in an appropriate order.

#5 Think about marketing related tasks. What materials do you need to prepare in order to market the LMS to its users?

To begin, work with your LMS vendor to determine a target date for the LMS to become available to your learners. Then create a timeline to complete the below tasks.

- Determine a name for the new LMS.

- Create an LMS logo.
- Determine a multi-tier marketing plan for different employee levels.
- Draft the look of the user interface.
- Add gamification elements, if needed.
- Create an LMS introductory video, emails, or posters to help you internally market the system.

#6 Here are some other, more generalized tasks you might like to add to your implementation plan.

Remember, you can download a spreadsheet of these tasks by joining the LinkedIn group referred to at the front of this book! Also, ask your LMS vendor if they have a standard set of tasks you can incorporate into your plan.

- Decide how many administrator levels are needed, with associated permissions.
- Create a list of tasks each level of administrator will complete.
- Decide on lead administrators for each department, if your organization is large.
- Determine a "regular chores" list for administrators.
- Create an LMS support email address that routes to the administrator group.
- Will IT have an administrator role in the new LMS?

- Determine what systems will integrate with the LMS. Maybe your HRIS?
- Decide on a go-live date for the LMS.
- Discuss ADA 508 compliance. How will your organization ensure the LMS and its associated content is accessible to everyone?
- Run a test batch import of all data types, such as course history, user information, and so on. (Ask your LMS vendor for advice.)
- After running successful test batches, import all data. Test to confirm success. (Again, this task will be completed with your vendor's help.)
- Discuss whether the interface should be offered in multiple languages.
- Create course equivalencies.
- Explore the benefits of xAPI, and how it can be effectively introduced.
- Get administrator "how to" documents from your vendor, if possible.
- Discuss how to utilize assessments and surveys more effectively.
- Schedule super administrator training with your LMS vendor.
- Explore security features and any national or international regulations pertaining to the data in your LMS.
- Negotiate the contract. (Check out the LinkedIn group for up to date information on how to negotiate your contract.

LMS contracts change based on industry trends, so it's better to address that information outside of this book.)

- Negotiate an SLA, or Service Level Agreement. (See YouTube channel Learn Tech Collective for advice on negotiating a SLA.)
- Decide when to cut over from your old LMS to the new LMS.
- Communicate that cut-over plan to your end users.
- Decide on the URL for the new LMS.
- Replace links to the old LMS with links to the new one.
- Train administrators on new system processes.
- Begin weekly recorded webinars on LMS administration targeted for different admin levels.
- Begin bi-weekly LMS "office hours," to assist your LMS administrators with data entry and basic questions.
- Develop how-to videos for common LMS user/administrator tasks.
- Evaluate your organization's training data entry procedure and streamline it. (Make sure your trainers track their classroom sessions and attendees in the LMS.)
- Test user interface prior to go-live. (Have lots of people test it. Try to break it.)
- Test class scheduling functionality.
- Test learning tracks or paths, and reports.
- Test upload of courses.
- Test EVERYTHING.
- Allow extra time to troubleshoot.

- Run a test of the system backup, if there is one.
- Run a test upgrade.
- System FAQ documents for members of your IT department as well as end users. (Definitely explain how to reset a user password, if passwords are required!)
- Review current third-party course vendors. Do you want to purchase e-learning content from these vendors, or would you rather create your own going forward?

MARKETING TIPS

You think your new system is pretty cool, but will your employees feel the same? Consider how you are going to market your system's many benefits and features to your employee base. Pretend that you are marketing a new product, and think of some creative ways to present the system to employees, supervisors, and executive leadership. Heck, you may even want to restructure your training program in order to take full advantage of your system.

#1

Get your leadership on board early!

By leadership, I mean all levels – supervisors, mid-level leadership, executive leadership, the works. These important stakeholders can make or break your LMS rollout. In order to win the support of a stakeholder, you must learn to think like one. That means realizing what information leadership will want from you in order to feel secure that the LMS is going to benefit the organization.

As discussed earlier in the book, it is important to fully understand leadership's goals for the system. Once you understand their goals, devise a clever plan as to how you will show leadership that the system is meeting their expectations.

Here are some strategies to promote the LMS to leadership:

- Research and share with your leadership how many similarly-sized companies have an LMS. (Ask your vendor.)
- Estimate how much the system will save you in expenses by reducing the amount of instructor-led training.
- An LMS makes it easier for the company to grow and still deliver quality training in multiple locations! Always great to point out!
- Need more ways to "sell" your system's success? Check out the last chapter of this book or ask for advice in the LinkedIn group.

- Brainstorm more ideas with your training department and LMS vendor. If you need graphics to present the system's benefits, speak with your marketing department.

What are three specific ways you will show leadership the benefits or advantages of the learning management system?

#2 Create internal marketing campaigns months in advance of the system roll-out.

So, you devised a brilliant LMS marketing scheme aimed at company leadership. They think the system is a stupendous idea and you're a genius. Bravo. You can now start Marketing Phase Two: Selling the system to everyone who will actually use it.

You're probably saying, "Hold on... won't they just adapt to the system once we roll it out?" Maybe. It depends on whether your employees are tech-savvy, and whether they are accustomed to navigating online courses. It also depends on how many employees you have. If you have a large employee base, it's better to begin communicating about your learning management system early through colorful emails and back-of-house posters.

The key is to advertise the system's EXCITING BENEFITS! Will the system save employees time? Make mandatory classes easier and more fun? Will it help employees achieve promotions? Tell employees when the system will be available and be sure you make your deadline. If you hit these points, tell employees when to expect the system, and make your marketing materials fun, you will capture your employees' curiosity. This will make it much easier to train everyone on using the LMS when the time comes.

In addition to pointing out the glitz and glamor of the new system, remember that learners will appreciate having a system that makes it easier for them to find relevant training content quickly. After all, who wants to spend five minutes clicking around in order to find a five-minute video? An LMS that is well organized and easy to use will help learners get the most out of their development time, so let them know how easy the LMS will be for them to use.

What are three exciting LMS benefits that you are going to share with your employee base?

#3 Tailor your marketing materials for each employee level, including leadership, executive leadership, etc.

As with any marketing campaign, you will need different sets of internal marketing materials for different levels of company leadership. Consider what each level will want to know about the LMS. Your executive leadership wants to know the company's investment in the LMS is justified. What metrics do they need in order to show a return on investment?

You are going to spend time training employees on the LMS. Consider how to show the value of that training time to mid-level managers and supervisors. The more voices you have in support of the learning management system, the easier it will be to integrate into your company.

Write down ways that you will market the LMS to each of three levels: employee base, mid-level managers, and executive leadership.

3

Assembling the Administrator Team

Have you raised a teenager? I haven't. But I know through keen observation that learning management systems closely resemble pouty, angsty adolescents. Your LMS just needs some bright blue hair, and it would be all set for high school.

You will need a strong administrator team to teach the LMS the difference between right and wrong. Let's discuss the brave team that will guide your system's growth.

Defining Administrator Roles

Your administrator team can make or break your learning management system! Ensuring you have an effective team in place from the get-go, and supporting your admin team's training, are important steps you can take to promote your system's success.

#1 Consider what traits you want to see in your LMS administrators.

System administrators are some of my favorite people. They are incredibly special and long-suffering – kind of like the nuns of the IT world.

The term "administrator" can be used in a lot of different ways in relation to an LMS. An administrator can be anyone from a "super" administrator, who controls the system and is responsible for other administrators, to a lower-level administrator who runs data reports and performs analysis. You may have several levels of administrators, or you may simply have one super administrator if you are a small company.

You should decide early on in your implementation how many administrator levels you will need. More on this later in the section.

For now, here are traits to look for in administrator candidates:

- **Customer service prowess.** In the beginning, your admins will hear the same technical support question at least five times a day. They absolutely MUST be good-natured about providing answers. Your administrators are a critical part of helping employees get comfortable with the system – they are the face of your LMS.

- **Multi-tasking ability.** Speaking of questions, your admins need to be able to answer them while executing a broad range of tasks. Follow-through on tasks is important. Without thorough, regular maintenance, your system is going to slowly melt into a puddle of slime.
- **Technical knowledge.** Administrators are “catch-all” people, meaning they are expected to know everything about everything in their system. If they don't know it, they need to be willing to learn it with a minimum of encouragement and hand-holding.
- **Communication talents.** Also known as “technical telepathy.” Being able to evaluate the person asking you a question, discern what it is they are truly looking for, and provide them with an answer they can follow given their level of technical knowledge. It doesn't sound easy. And it's not as easy as it sounds.
- **Discretion.** Especially higher-level admins. They’re going to be seeing user data, possibly even personal addresses, and employment information. Either be sure your system does not include this information or be sure your admins are trustworthy.
- **Strong understanding of Murphy's Law.** “If it can go wrong, it will go wrong.” The more complex the LMS, the more opportunities there are for incredibly creative

problems to arise. Your admins need to have a sense of humor.

Are there other traits you want in your system administrators? Write them down. Also, write down the names of three to five people in your company who 1) may make good LMS administrators and 2) would be available to perform the role. If there is no one who is appropriate, write down the names of some people who have personal attributes that are close to what you would want in an administrator. Use these people as "templates" when you are looking for your administrators.

#2 Define the structure of your administrator team.

If you are a small company, an administrator team of four to five people may be all you need to manage your LMS. If you are a large company of several thousand, you will want a larger super administrator team (with unrestricted permissions), as well as a lower level of administrators who have restricted permissions. (In other words, they can't push any buttons that would cause the system to self-destruct.)

Additional administrators can take the strain off of your super administrator team by performing basic tasks, such as running data reports and answering basic technical support questions from users. Spreading out the workload frees up your super administrator team to handle complex technical issues and further develop the system.

Take a look at the following example of an administrator team structure. You might add or remove layers depending on your company's size.

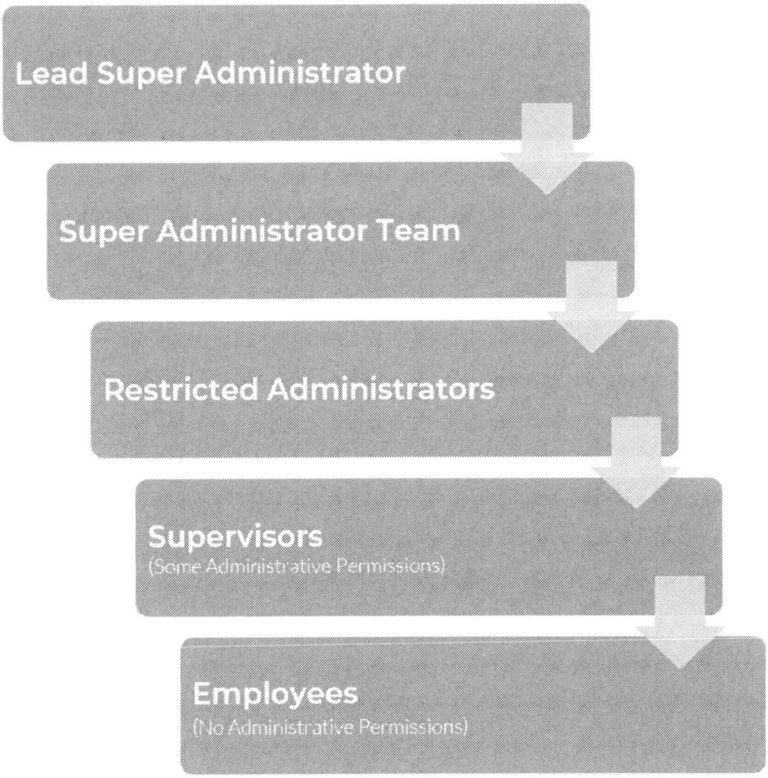

Sketch the structure of your administrator team and non-admin levels. Use the graphic provided above as a reference. Add additional levels if needed.

Your LMS Administrator Team's Structure

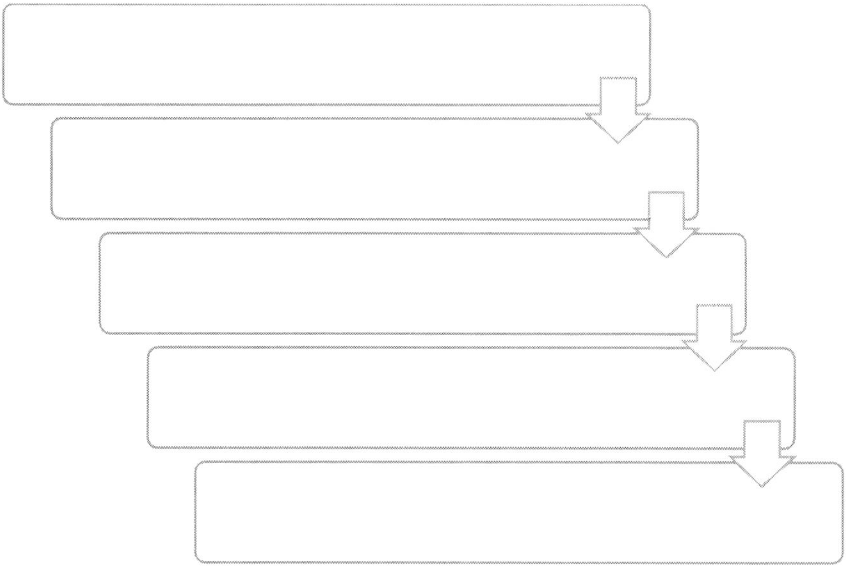

Review the information you gathered from your LMS vendor earlier in the book regarding typical tasks they suggest for system administrators. For each level of administrator, you listed above, write down a few tasks the admin level will handle.

#3 Other than your administrator team, who will directly help with implementation and maintenance of the LMS?

Your administrator team will likely be augmented by members of your IT department, especially during the implementation. For instance, it's common to have a database administrator assisting with system integrations. Members of your security team will evaluate any data vulnerabilities presented by the LMS. If your IT department has individuals who are dedicated to internal communications or change management, they will play a role in managing the speed and appearance of the implementation. While these individuals will be especially involved during the implementation, you are likely to still need them occasionally once the LMS is up and running. You might have a number of IT personnel involved in testing the LMS following implementation.

If you aren't sure what tasks you should perform to test your LMS, check out free resources available through the LinkedIn group.

Your LMS vendor will play a key role in assembling a timeline of implementation tasks. Some tasks will require your organization to take certain actions, some will require action from the vendor, and some items will require collaboration between you. Just as you rely on the vendor to have their personnel available to you in order to complete tasks on time, they will rely on you for the same.

It's important to have a project manager during the implementation who directs traffic and interfaces with the LMS vendor regarding what needs to happen and when. This person will also coordinate internal resources and deliverables from your organization in order to keep the project running on schedule.

In many cases, the person who will ultimately serve as the LMS super administrator also serves as the project manager, which leads right into our next section.

#4 Someone has to lead the charge!

It's time to choose a point-person to lead the LMS! Maybe that person will be you, or maybe you have someone in mind from your training team or IT department. If your company has multiple divisions or regions, you may need an admin team and point-person in each division, with one lead overseeing all divisions.

So, what does a super administrator look like?

It's kind of difficult to quantify a super admin. They should have a true conviction and passion for what they do. Have you seen Star Wars? Picture your LMS as the Millennium Falcon. It has lots of capabilities, but it's a little unstable and cranky. Your lead super administrator needs to be Han Solo – someone who cleverly persuades the system to do your company's bidding.

A lead super admin has all of the skills of a typical administrator, with a few more added on top.

- **Creativity** as it pertains to system functions. Super administrators are expected to have answers to every system-related question, even those that have never been asked before.
- **Critical thinking.** Having technical knowledge and following instructions is not enough. The ability to think through a problem and create a solution is important.
- **Communication with leadership.** Your lead super admin will be the figurehead for the LMS. This person will interface with a number of different levels within your company. He or she should be comfortable speaking with all levels of leadership, employees, and people outside the company, namely your LMS vendor. This person should be able to discern what level of information is appropriate for each party. For instance, they will normally provide top-

level information to executives, and technical support to employees.

- **Conviction.** Like any leader, a lead super administrator will encounter conflict. Having a bit of a backbone is important.
- **Ability to handle technical issues.** By "technical issues," we're talking major ones, like when the entire system goes belly up. And by "handle," I mean facilitate solutions without clouding up and raining. Sometimes it's very tempting.

Out of the potential administrators you wrote down earlier in this section, is there someone who stands out as a potential super administrator?

Write that person's name here:

#5

Your lead super admin needs a sidekick!

If your company has multiple regions or divisions, you may need a super administrator team for each region. It follows that you will want a lead super administrator to guide each of these teams. You may also want a "back-up" lead, who is responsible for the region or division's administrator functions when the lead is unavailable.

Lead super administrators and their back-ups should work closely and present a united approach to their administrator teams. Back-ups will ideally have the same skill set as lead super administrators, or they should be working toward it. It helps if each back-up is trained by their lead super administrator. That way, the lead and back-up will be on the same page regarding admin responsibilities, and they will provide the same training information and technical support to the administrator team.

Being a back-up is an awesome learning experience. I speak from experience! The position taught me far more about LMS administration than any book can. (Yes, including this one!)

As you can imagine, having a back-up for your lead super admin is useful for a variety of reasons. First, you need someone available in case your lead super admin is unavailable to perform their duties. Back-ups can assist your lead with admin tasks that require advanced knowledge and high-level system permissions. I've worked with brilliant back-ups who offer amazing ideas and support administrators by providing one-on-one training.

Having an extra hand is particularly helpful when there is a system issue that requires a speedy response, such as an outage. The back-ups I've worked with have been a huge help during such issues, coming up with solutions and handling half of the technical support.

It isn't strictly necessary to have back-ups in place during your system implementation, although it is nice to have the extra help. Your lead super administrator may want to pick their back-up after evaluating their administrator team for the best possible candidate.

One final thought: Ideally, the back-up should respect your lead super administrator's vision for the LMS. You don't want two conflicting voices leading the system.

If applicable, write the names of some possible back-ups.

#6 What permissions will be needed for each level of system administrator?

You will assign permissions to each administrator level within your LMS, assuming your platform allows you to define them. (Some learning management systems have predefined permissions for different administrator levels.) Permissions define which areas of the LMS a user can access or modify. For instance, a lower-level administrator may only have access to run data reports. A higher-level admin may be able to run reports AND modify the associated data.

The permissions you assign to admins will depend upon how much access you want them to have. Permissions will also be based on the tasks assigned to each level of administrator. Consider whether you want IT to have the ability to reset LMS passwords. Decide on your permissions levels early on in the

implementation process and discuss them with your vendor.

Make notes of admin permissions levels here.

#7 How will IT be involved with the LMS after the implementation? Are they part of your admin team? In what capacity?

In some companies, the IT department makes up part or all of the LMS super administrator team. In other companies, IT does not maintain the system, but they do assist when employees need their passwords reset. If you have many employees and the LMS will require them to enter a password, consider giving members of IT the permissions needed to reset passwords. This will take part of the technical support load off of your LMS administrators. Explore these possibilities with your IT team before the system comes online, so you have technical support in place.

By the way, you can avoid the password reset issue entirely by enabling single sign-on (SSO). Discuss this with your vendor. If SSO is enabled, the LMS will not require the user to enter an ID or password. The LMS will pull the user's information from somewhere else, often their Windows authentication.

Speak with your company's IT department. Will they provide technical support for LMS users? If so, what type of support will they provide?

#8 Who will enter training data? How many hours of data entry will each administrator perform per week?

One major function of your learning management system is to record and store data related to your company's training. It is important that your training data is as accurate and complete as possible. Training data is not only used for tracking employee progress. It can also be used for legal purposes. For example, delivering compliance-related courses and tracking their completion can support your company's due diligence toward injury prevention, ensuring proper employee conduct, and so on.

Your training data will be entered in one of two ways – automatically or manually. In the case of e-learning courses delivered through your LMS, training data will be recorded automatically. Let's say an employee goes into your learning management system and completes a course. The system will record that that employee took the course and it will appear on the employee's transcript.

Let's say the same employee attends an instructor-led, classroom-style course. Obviously, there is no way for the LMS to know that the employee was in the classroom. The instructor, or some other party, will need to enter the employee's attendance into the LMS after the class is complete. This is what is known as manually entering training data.

If your company is large and offers many instructor-led classes, the manual entry of training data can require a significant amount of work. You will want to identify early on which parties will be responsible for the entry of this data. You may want to give all company trainers the permissions necessary to enter training data.

Your super administrator team will want to create data entry guidelines and use these guidelines to teach those entering data how to complete the process accurately. The data entry guidelines will vary depending on which LMS you choose, as entry processes vary widely.

Ask your LMS vendor if there are any processes or add-on systems that will make data entry more efficient. Some companies have created custom tools to speed up manual data entry. There is a video in the LinkedIn group that demonstrates a way to quickly create training data import spreadsheets, assuming your LMS uses them.

You may be surprised how many hours your administrators will spend entering data into your system. For example, I have experience with a Fortune 500 company that has hundreds of administrators, many of whom spend at least eight hours a week entering data. I was able to implement a data entry process that saved many hours per admin per week. The estimated savings for that company was **hundreds of thousands of dollars per year**! (See the above LinkedIn group video for details!) It is worth your time to explore options that will make your data entry more efficient.

Jot down applicable notes about your data entry process, how much data you expect, and who will be entering it. If your company previously had an LMS, how many hours per week did administrators spend entering data? Do you expect this amount to increase or decrease?

Training the Administrator Team

Without training, your LMS admins are just a bunch of nerds with a lot of potential. Give your nerds some knowledge, and they will become dangerously productive. When you are first implementing your system, be sure your admins receive the tools they need to understand the LMS. When new admins join the team, they should receive the same in-depth training as those in the initial team.

#1 How will your lead super administrator be trained?

When you are discussing the system implementation with your LMS vendor, ask if they will train your lead super administrator for free. Super admin training may take days and cost a significant amount.

If the expense of this initial training comes out of your company's pocket, it's still worth it! This is the time to dip into your petty cash and sell a couple of office chairs.

Your lead super administrator will be called upon to fix obscure problems, explain odd behavior, and read the system's tea leaves, sometimes without assistance from your vendor. Give your lead super admin the benefit of in-depth LMS classes, then have them pass their knowledge along to the rest of your administrator team. If you have already chosen a back-up lead, provide them with the same in-depth training.

What will it cost to have your lead(s) trained by your vendor? How many days will the training take?

#2 How will your other super admins be trained?

Once the lead super administrator has received LMS training, will he or she pass that knowledge along to the rest of your super admin team? Better yet, will the vendor offer training to the entire group?

Your LMS vendor may be willing to offer a group rate to train all of your super administrators in one session. If this group rate is reasonable, it may be effective to train all administrators at one time. Otherwise, your lead super admin is likely the best option for training. This will be an excellent test of the lead super administrator's grasp of the system!

You may want to divide the super administrator training into multiple sessions, due to the amount of information that your admins will need to digest. It is not unusual for super administrator training to take place over the course of three to four days. For a lower-level administrator, a one-day training may be sufficient, or even two to three hours.

Jot down your plan for training your super administrator team. If you would like to hear how other organizations have handled their administrator training, post a question in the LinkedIn group.

#3 How will you train your other levels of administrators? Will you provide classroom training or virtual sessions?

Once your super administrator team is trained, you can choose a strategy to acquaint the rest of your admins with the LMS. Admin training can be done virtually or in person.

When choosing a training strategy for the rest of your LMS administrators, consider where they are located. Are all of your admins working at the same office, or are they spread out across multiple locations? Some companies have many locations with one admin at each. For these companies, a virtual admin training is practical.

If you choose to do classroom-style training, it is ideal to have a computer available for each of your participants. If your participants do not have laptops they can bring along, try renting a group of laptops from a local technology company. The cost is minimal for a couple of days, and your participants will get a lot more out of the training if they are able to use the system hands-on.

The ideal admin training includes an explanation of each basic task the administrator group will be asked to perform. Each task can be followed by an exercise that allows class participants to complete the task on their own. Super administrators should be available to offer assistance when participants need it. If you are doing classroom-style training, super administrators can simply walk around and offer support to anyone who is struggling. If you are offering a virtual admin training, you can have your super administrators available by instant messaging or phone for one-on-one support. Be sure to hold the initial administrator training close to the system's roll-out date so the information stays fresh in everyone's minds.

Virtual admin training can be very effective and efficient. I once trained a group of over 200 administrators in three hours using a virtual training application. I demonstrated basic system tasks, then had participants attempt each task before moving on. During the training, there were super administrators standing by to take participant questions through IM. I was also available for Q&A after the class was finished. The Q&A session lasted nearly the length of the class and allowed participants to begin working on more complex tasks while still receiving support.

One training will not be enough! Follow-up sessions will be needed to train new administrators and refresh existing admins. Providing a solid initial session gets everyone off on the right foot and makes follow-up training much easier.

Will you use classroom training or virtual sessions to train administrators beneath the super admin level? Do you want to complete the training in one session or several? Jot your ideas here.

#4 Train supervisors on management-level features and benefits. Teach in terms of "how this benefits you."

Talk to your LMS vendor. Are there tools in your LMS that are specifically designed for leadership? For instance, supervisors may be able to assign and approve classes for their team and check what assignments team members have completed. You may want to create a strategy for training company leadership on how to make use of these features. If you expect leadership to learn how to perform specific tasks, communicate that consistently from the beginning of your system implementation. If you don't want to do full training sessions for leadership, you will want to at least create some internal marketing pieces with them in mind, showing the system's benefits.

Supervisors are often concerned that implementing an LMS will make certain tasks harder to complete. For example, if you are using the LMS to collect electronic signatures from employees, it may take longer than collecting written signatures, depending on how many computers are available to employees. If you have one computer and forty employees in a particular department, it may be difficult to have all of those employees log onto the LMS for long periods of time. This is something for your super administrator team to consider. If needed, you can limit the length of classes delivered through the LMS, or reduce the number of classes that are assigned at a given time. When speaking with leadership about the system implementation, make it clear that you are evaluating each department's needs, and modifying your approach as necessary.

Share the positive pay-offs of the LMS:

- Providing training on-demand, whenever an employee has time
- Increasing employee retention through games and interesting content
- Offering a broader range of training
- Eliminating paper in favor of digital documents
- Making it easier to track compliance training

Managing the Administrator Team Effectively

Maintaining a learning management system is an ongoing project. There are a variety of "daily chores" that contribute to system maintenance, as well as one-time projects intended to develop the system or its content. (We'll talk about these projects soon.) Making sure that tasks are juggled and prioritized appropriately should be the responsibility of your lead super administrator. Below are some ideas that may help in managing your learning management system tasks.

#1 Assemble a list of tasks each administrator level will perform on a routine basis.

As with any system, an LMS requires ongoing maintenance. Your lead super administrator will want to assemble a list of necessary tasks for each level of admin, to make sure nothing gets overlooked. For super administrators, tasks could include the development of course materials, the uploading of course content, periodic clean-up of data, the creation of new permissions levels, and other tasks completed on a regular basis. For administrators below the super admin level, there may be ongoing tasks associated with pulling data reports or providing basic technical support.

Your lead super administrator should have a strong idea of what tasks go on a "regular chores list" after several weeks of system experience. There will be maintenance tasks that are specific to your system. Ask your LMS vendor for tasks that they would suggest your admins complete on a regular basis. They should also be able to give you an idea of how often these tasks should be completed.

In the early stages of system implementation, most LMS tasks will fall to your lead super administrator or super admin team. Tasks during implementation may include importing data into the system, creating courses, running initial training data reports, and the like.

Below, list at least five recurring tasks, how often these tasks should be completed, and which admin level should complete them. If desired, share these tasks in the LinkedIn group and ask others what tasks they complete regularly.

#2 Create a quarterly list of projects to be completed.

It's easier to manage an LMS by looking at it as a big project, made up of many smaller projects. It will benefit your administrator team to have a list of LMS projects with corresponding time frames. Your lead super administrator should generate this project list on a periodic basis. Tasks should be broken into chunks if necessary and assigned to groups or individual admins.

Here are some examples of small projects an administrator group could tackle.

- Create a catalog of all LMS courses, divided by subject matter.
- Run an audit of all training data twice a year. Check data for accuracy. Was it entered correctly? Are instructors filling in all of the fields you want?
- Create an annual summary of training data that goes to company leadership. Great for marketing the LMS!
- Create a specific course for the LMS. As any e-learning developer can tell you, one course may represent hundreds of work hours, so each course is certainly its own project.
- Do a visual makeover of the employee home page or other frequently-accessed LMS pages.

Have your lead super administrator generate a list of projects. When appropriate, communicate the project list to the administrator team.

The project list should include the following:

- A description of each project
- Who will lead the project, and who will participate
- Approximate start and end dates

See the Learn Tech Collective materials for a project list template.

#3 Communicate projects and tasks effectively to the administrator team.

Once your lead super administrator has a list of regular chores and special projects, it's time to figure out how to communicate all of the tasks to the administrator team. There are many ways to do this. You can use Microsoft Project, draw a flow chart, or create a checklist to send by email.

Once a project list has been created, post it in appropriate places, such as the boss's office, teamwork area, or SharePoint. Make it colorful and fun! It may be practical to insert the list into an email, and send it to your administrator team periodically.

#4 If LMS administrators are working at multiple locations, create a regular check-in procedure.

If all of your admins are working in the same office, it's pretty easy to keep tabs on how projects are going. You just use the Cubicle Telephone Game.

> **Lead Super Admin** (shouts over cubicle wall): *Hey Bob, how's that course coming?*
>
> **Bob**: *My part's done. Want me to ask Jose in the next cubicle where he's at with his deadline?*

Works just fine when you're all in the same place, but it's not unusual to have administrators working out of multiple locations. If your team is working out of more than one office, you will want to create a regular check-in procedure. This check-in procedure can be as simple as a weekly email to the lead super administrator detailing what each member of the team has accomplished. The lead super administrator can compile the main tasks that have been completed and let the administrator team know the status of major projects. Check-ins can also be performed by phone or through in-person meetings, whatever is practical. The goal is to have frequent and effective communication regarding the status of all projects under the LMS umbrella. You may also want to gather your super administrators together on at least a quarterly or bi-annual basis for deeper discussions.

How will the administrator team check in with your lead super administrator? How often will they check in, and what information will be provided during each check-in?

#5 Should the super administrator team have their own email distribution list?

Creating an administrator distribution list would allow employees to email all super admins via one email address. For example, let's say Renee, Nicole, and Tracie are on your super admin team. An employee could email the super admins using LMSSupport@yourcompany.com, and their message would go to all three super admins. This helps speed up responses to technical support inquiries since multiple people receive each message. The address can be listed on the LMS employee home page in case employees need assistance. It can also be listed at the bottom of posters advertising the LMS to employees.

If you are creating a distribution list, write the email address here:

If you are not creating a distribution list, how will employees contact your administrators for technical support? Write this below. If desired, ask for ideas in the LinkedIn group.

Additional Tips

It is important that company leadership support your LMS, especially when you are first introducing the LMS to employees. Make an effort to turn members of leadership into enthusiastic proponents of the system. What can the LMS do for your leaders? Additionally, what can the system do for individual departments within your company?

#1 Get supervisors involved in their team's training progress.

Does your company's culture encourage supervisors to be enthusiastic about their team's training progress? If not, the implementation of your LMS is an opportunity to get supervisors on board with your company training program. One easy way to get supervisors to pay attention to the LMS is through competition! For example, release training data summaries showing which departments in your company are conducting the most training. Many learning management systems offer gamification features, such as leaderboards and other ranking tools. Another great call-out could be the impact of safety training on your Workers Comp statistics. Have claims decreased as the amount of safety training increased?

You can send out these summaries to company leadership specifically congratulating top-performing teams, and giving prizes if appropriate. If you can get your company leadership on board with this process, and have them comment and congratulate the "winning" teams, it will motivate departments with lower numbers to step up.

The easiest way to get leadership behind the system is to continuously showcase how it benefits them. If you can do anything to save leadership time by implementing particular classes or documents in the system, do so early on.

#2 Anticipate that leadership will resist the LMS in the beginning.

Until company leadership sees what the system is capable of, expect to encounter resistance. If your company is technophobic, you may have an especially challenging time! Find tangible ways to show the system's value to those who oppose it.

Let's say your Customer Service Vice President is your loudest opponent. Look for a way you can use the system to solve an issue for the Customer Service department. Maybe you can create a fun, interactive cashier training that helps new cashiers retain PLUs for faster check-outs. Show your VP a mock-up of the course before you create it. Once it's finished, have him/her give the class a whirl! Implement the class, get some solid data on how much retention has improved, and provide the data to your VP. If you consistently approach system opponents with this problem-solving attitude, they will come to appreciate the system and rely on your admin team for solutions.

Trying to get new LMS administrators on board? Some people are "forced" into their LMS role. Be prepared to enthusiastically explain the benefits of the system! It is important that every administrator and member of the training team present a positive outlook of the system to other employees.

#3 Will multiple departments contribute content to the learning management system?

Let's say you work for a retail company with multiple departments. Depending on your company and industry, two employees working in two different departments may receive a completely different set of training. If your company delivers a lot of department-specific training, you will most likely want a "training content advisor" from each of your company's departments. This person can help you effectively cater to the department's training needs by telling you what training content is most useful to them. You may want this person to also be a member of the LMS administrator team.

Identify possible "training content advisors" from each company department. Write their names and corresponding departments below.

#4 Make sure the LMS administrators communicate effectively with other teams who are involved with the LMS.

No administrator operates in a bubble, so it's important to keep stakeholders outside of the admin team apprised of system updates, changes to the catalog, and the like. Be sure to decide:

- Which organizational groups need to know about specific tasks, such as upgrades or system downtime?
- Who in the administrator team is responsible for communicating these updates, and what delivery method will they use?
- Who specifically will receive these updates?
- How often?

Check in with the organizational groups who will receive these updates, so they know what to expect from the LMS administrator team.

4

Types of Training Content & Course Creation Resources

It's all well and good to have a learning management system, but it's pretty silly to have a system with no training content. In order for an LMS to be successful, a wide range of e-learning materials will need to be developed. Content may include documents, videos, games, interactive modules, assessments, and more. With e-learning content comes the need for course creation tools, some of which are listed in this section to help you get started.

Strange Acronyms and What They Mean

This is by no means an exhaustive list... there are lots of weird LMS terms that you will encounter when creating course content. Just pretend you work for NASA. That's probably the only organization with a similar number of acronyms.

#1 SCORM (Sharable Content Object Reference Model)

Rustici Software, a manufacturer of SCORM compliance products, has an easy-to-understand definition of SCORM. Here's what they have to say:

> *"SCORM is a set of technical standards for e-learning software products. SCORM tells programmers how to write their code so that it can 'play well' with other e-learning software. It is the de facto industry standard for e-learning interoperability. Specifically, SCORM governs how online learning content and Learning Management Systems (LMSs) communicate with each other."*

So, what does SCORM mean to you? Depends on your LMS. Talk to your LMS vendor about the standards used by your learning management system. These standards will influence how course content is built.

For the nerds among us... SCORM was originally developed by ADL (Advanced Distributed Learning) over ten years ago. SCORM uses JS API to bridge communication between the LMS and course content. Rustici Software gives a longer definition of SCORM with examples, as well as excellent SCORM resources. Visit them here:

www.scorm.com/scorm-explained/

#2 Experience API/xAPI

As we discussed previously, SCORM has been around for a long time. xAPI, formerly known as Tin Can API, is essentially the next generation of SCORM. And yes, the two terms do refer to the same thing.

If you were wondering, API stands for "Application Program Interface." An API essentially lets operating systems and other computer programs talk to each other and share data.

Rustici Software has an excellent definition of the Experience API:

> *"The Experience API (or xAPI) is a new specification for learning technology that makes it possible to collect data about the wide range of experiences a person has (online and offline). This API captures data in a consistent format about a person or group's activities from many technologies. Very different systems are able to securely communicate by capturing and sharing this stream of activities using xAPI's simple vocabulary."*

In other words, xAPI extends beyond a learning management system and allows you to pull learning-related information from other systems! Cool! Ask your LMS vendor if their system accommodates xAPI, and if so, in what ways you can use it to your company's advantage.

Find out more about xAPI from Rustici Software:

https://xapi.com/overview/

#3 AICC (Aviation Industry Computer-Based Training Committee)

Like SCORM, AICC refers to a collection of standards that govern development, delivery, and evaluation of courses delivered through technology. Both SCORM and AICC help the LMS communicate with course content. They are almost like interpreters, bridging the language gap between people from two different countries.

Don't be fooled by the incredibly long name. AICC is actually used by technology-based training professionals outside of the aviation industry. Your LMS may conform to AICC standards. Ask your LMS vendor what effect, if any, these standards will have on your course content development.

If you're curious, AICC uses HACP (HTTP AICC Communication Protocol) to facilitate communication between course content and the LMS. Do you need to know that? Not really. But now you have one more acronym that you can drop around your co-workers. Actually, an acronym within an acronym.

#4 So, which is better for an LMS to use, SCORM or AICC?

Ask your LMS vendor. It depends on your situation and what you need the LMS to track.

If you need a secure connection for the LMS, your only option is AICC. SCORM uses JavaScript to connect, and JavaScript doesn't accommodate secure connections.

AICC also allows you to store the LMS and course content on the same server, whereas SCORM is hindered by cross-browser scripting problems. (It is not critical that you understand what cross-browser scripting is. But you should ask your LMS vendor if it will be an issue.)

Many e-learning development tools, such as Articulate's applications, allow you to easily publish content that is compliant with both SCORM and AICC.

#5 Everything you've said in this section went whistling over my head like a bat out of hell.

That's okay! You don't need to become a programmer to understand how an LMS works. The terms in this section are provided as references that you may need in order to discuss system specifications with your vendor. If you want more information, or if you have specific questions, you can post in the LinkedIn group.

If you've looked at all of this and concluded that the last thing you want to do is develop content for the LMS, that's okay too. There are many companies who will develop course content for you and provide technical support, so you won't ever have to look at another acronym again. If you would like company referrals, feel free to ask in our LinkedIn group.

BLENDED LEARNING

Instructor-led classes don't need to take place in a classroom! Consider conducting classes through web conferencing, conference calls, and other creative formats. Virtual classroom tools allow you to conduct a live class effectively and engage your employees.

#1 Prepare your learners to accept "new" formats of training. Begin introducing them to new delivery methods.

As you explore your new LMS, look for ways to replace small pieces of classroom content with videos, documents, or simulations.

Start with the obvious, the easy, and the accessible. Viewing YouTube videos costs nothing, and you can link to them in the LMS. Are there quick reference guides or internal communications you can repurpose into learning? Earmark these items to be placed into the LMS once it's available.

Remember that no training has to be one hundred percent computer-based, or entirely classroom based. In your virtual classes, include activities where learners do research online or do scavenger hunts around the office, before returning to class to share their findings. Rather than accomplishing everything in the classroom, find other ways to deliver content, before and after class. Look for ways to cut material out of classroom training and replace with other resources.

Add mentoring activities to your classes, where a learner consults with an expert to gather research or seek advice. Look for existing resources in your organization - supervisors, subject matter experts (SMEs), and experienced employees, especially those seeking a promotion. Look for topics in your program that can be reinforced through coaching and one-on-one interactions. Reward those who teach others by making mentoring a line item on job performance reviews.

Blending together different delivery methods will be engaging for your learners, but it may initially be frightening for your learning and development team. Those who only know classroom training will be required to learn new skills, such as e-learning development, video production, and technical editing. Those on your team who see change as exciting will dance. Those who fear technology will hide. But change is real and necessary. Change happens regardless of whether we ask for it. And the change to blended learning is spreading across the entire learning and development industry.

Is there a specific course or initiative you would like to present in a blended format? Write the name of the course. If desired, share your idea in the LinkedIn group and ask for feedback.

Web Conferencing

#2

Blackboard Collaborate, Adobe Connect, and Zoom are some tools that allow you to deliver live, virtual training through web conferencing. Such tools provide built-in phone conferencing with VoIP audio. I've done a lot of virtual classes with large attendee lists, and have found it to be a great way to engage an audience.

Web conferencing platforms often provide the following tools.

- Video recordings of each session for later playback
- An interactive whiteboard
- Public and private chats
- Easy user management tools
- Annotation tools so users can revise a document or make notes as a group
- "Breakout rooms" so you can divide a class into smaller discussion groups
- Universal accessibility, including for those with disabilities
- Access to live web conferencing from a mobile device
- Support for international users

In order to retain employees' interest throughout a web conference, limit sessions to 45 minutes or less. If you plan to deliver longer classes through web conferencing, provide learners with frequent breaks and do your best to utilize all of the interactive functions of the meeting software. They will make your sessions that much more effective.

#3 Conference Calls

While conference calls aren't exactly virtual classes, they are an excellent way to disseminate information to employees at multiple locations. You have the drawback of not being able to present visuals, but participants are easily able to ask questions.

Here are some suggestions regarding conference call training.

- Keep calls short. By short, I mean twenty minutes or shorter if you can. Without visuals, your employees may find it difficult to stay focused.
- If you give training credit to those attending the call, remember to take attendance at the beginning or end of the session.
- At the beginning of the call, ask all participants to mute their phone lines. Explain how to unmute and let participants know they can do this to ask questions.
- If your company uses hold music, be sure to tell employees not to put your training session on hold! The last thing your call needs is a smarmy trumpet wailing in the background.

Screen Sharing

#4

Screen sharing software allows one user to view another user's computer screen remotely. In some cases, one user can take over another's screen. Web conferencing applications often include this type of tool, but there are also screen sharing tools on the market that are independent.

There are tons of ways to use this type of software for training and technical support! Screen sharing is especially useful when working one on one with a learner through a virtual environment. You can demonstrate how to use software applications and then pass control back to the learner so they can demonstrate what you've shown them.

Screen sharing applications often include the ability to chat, send files, and participate in sessions using various mobile devices.

Using the LinkedIn group, ask others what virtual classroom tools they use. Based on your research, what other virtual classroom tools would you like to explore?

Design Elements, Templates, and Tools

What's that you say? You have a fully-functional LMS and no course content? In order to speed up content creation, you can utilize design elements, templates, and tools that are available on the Internet. This section reviews some possible resources.

#1 eLearning Brothers Templates

eLearning Brothers has some excellent templates that will allow you to create training for your LMS without starting from scratch. They also have some great visual elements that are perfect for snazzing up instructor-led training. I've used their content for years.

Here is a partial list of the templates they offer:

- Customizable Pre-made Courses
- Games/Activities
- Cutout People
- Player Skins
- Page Layouts
- Graphics
- Sound Effects
- Adobe Captivate and Presenter Templates
- Articulate Studio and Storyline Templates
- Lectora Templates

To find out more about eLearning Brothers, visit their website:

www.elearningbrothers.com

Do some research on the Internet. What other template resources would you like to explore? If desired, use the LinkedIn group to ask for resource suggestions.

#2 Do your training PowerPoints have a cohesive look?

Implementing an LMS is a great excuse to update the look of your entire training program! If you haven't already, examine the PowerPoint templates that you are using for both instructor-led and e-learning classes. Do your presentations have a clean, consistent look? If not, maybe it's time to spruce up your materials. By the way, you can use PowerPoints to build e-learning classes using Adobe Captivate.

Do you have different levels of training (100-level, 200-level) or common subjects for most of your classes (Finance, Marketing)? Maybe you could color-code your PowerPoints and class materials by level or subject. For example, all of your technology class materials could be green. It makes for a nice effect when all of your materials can be visually categorized.

#3 Review existing training materials. Are the graphics and animations high-quality?

Maybe your existing materials are already in e-learning format, or maybe not. Either way, you can easily transform your existing content into LMS-friendly fare using Captivate and other programs! Transforming existing content will save you oodles of time, compared to creating courses from scratch.

The professionalism of your graphics and animations will make or break your e-learning content! Employees truly appreciate courses that are well thought out and visually stimulating. Ask yourself – would YOU want to look at your current training materials?

If your marketing department is not able to provide the visuals you need for training content, you might consider hiring a contractor or LMS administrator who has this particular skill set. If you just need a few fun illustrations, check out the online resources listed below.

Be sure to ask your marketing department whether there are specific corporate guidelines relating to graphics and animations.

Here are some online resources that can provide you with visual elements:

- www.shutterstock.com *(Photos, Illustrations, Vectors, Videos)*
- www.graphicriver.net *(Design, Textures, Vectors, Icons)*
- www.istockphoto.com *(Photos, Illustrations, Audio, Video)*

#4 Make presentations pop using fun fonts.

Fonts are an easy way to add some attitude to your training materials! Your company may already have proprietary fonts available – ask your marketing department what they have in their stockpile. There are also many fonts available for free or purchase on the Internet.

Just remember that if you use a non-standard font and then send materials to someone who doesn't have the font, they may have issues viewing your work. Be sure to send documents as PDFs and flatten PowerPoints to preserve their visual elements.

Here are some online resources for awesome fonts:

- www.1001freefonts.com *(Free)*
- www.google.com/fonts *(Free)*
- www.typekit.com *(Purchase)*
- www.fontsquirrel.com *(Free/Purchase)*

#5 Utilize tutorials and resources for building e-learning content.

If you are new to building e-learning courses, you may want to look at some tutorials and resources that will reduce your learning curve. The resources available online – for free – are extensive! I can testify as to the quality of freebie tutorials… I took design courses in college but got 70% of my software design know-how from Internet research.

For just about any software, there are YouTube videos showing step-by-step tutorials. Many software companies, such as TechSmith, provide websites that are chock-full of templates and tutorials. Software companies also offer help sections and discussion forums on their websites. If you ever get stuck due to a technical snafu, just Google your issue! When I was first learning video production, I ran across a rare glitch and quickly found the solution in a random discussion forum. The Internet is the perfect resource when you are looking for free, beginner-level information.

For comprehensive instructional design advice, check out *Design for How People Learn* by Julie Dirksen. It's an excellent read.

If you want to get a deeper knowledge of design in a short time, try taking a course at a local community college! Many colleges offer classes on common programs, such as Adobe and Microsoft, for a reasonable cost. You could also take some in-depth video tutorials, such as those available from LinkedIn Learning.

Software

If you are planning to develop your own virtual training content on behalf of your company, there are many software programs you can choose from. A few of my personal favorites are listed in this section. Also listed are some of the tools within your LMS that may help you develop content.

#1 eLearning Development Tools

Volumes have been written about development tools, so I won't go into extensive detail. If you're just starting to develop your own content and you would like to explore some application choices, check out Adobe Captivate and Articulate 360. Many learning organizations are either an "Adobe shop" or an "Articulate shop," meaning they specifically hire developers with knowledge of Captivate or Articulate. Understanding both will serve you well. That being said, your organization will likely not need licenses for both. Research the strengths and weaknesses of both options and try them for yourself, then choose the one that seems best for your needs.

I also personally recommend exploring:

- Other Adobe applications, such as Premiere Pro and Animate, for video content
- Camtasia for easy video editing
- WalkMe and Live Content Studio for interactive tutorials

If desired, ask the LinkedIn group for advice regarding development tools.

#2 Videos and Audio

One of the greatest benefits of an LMS is the ability to deliver training content through video. This is an excellent alternative to instructor-led training, as it is still highly engaging for employees, and can be more cost-effective than offering instructor-led courses.

Video production can be expensive. Speak with your marketing department to see if your company does in-house video production. If so, see if you can borrow the production equipment for the creation of training videos. If not, purchase a camera with decent customer reviews that suits your budget. You don't need Hollywood equipment to produce high-quality training videos.

However, equipment is only part of the battle. You still need to have a production lead who understands film and audio processes. There is a great deal of planning that goes into any successful film shoot, including the storyboarding of what content you want to cover and what shots will be most beneficial.

See if you can identify some individuals who can help you in the video production process. If there is no one available within your company to help, consider hiring a third-party production company. The other alternative is to identify someone within your company who has an interest in video production and get them the training they need to be successful in this role. Many community and career colleges offer classes on video production. Taking a basic film class is invaluable since it will introduce basic concepts, such as lighting, how to frame shots, and how to plan a shoot.

You may want to purchase Camtasia or Adobe Premiere in order to edit your videos. Both are relatively easy to learn and won't break the bank.

Be sure to check the hardware requirements of any software you purchase. Video production takes a lot of processing power, so you may need to purchase a laptop depending on what you are doing.

Great audio is key for e-learning courses, and it is much easier to produce than video. All you need to produce audio is a good microphone and basic audio editing software. I've used Adobe Audition for years. Audacity is an excellent free audio editing software that works for PCs and Macs.

If you are just starting out, you may want to assemble a mobile recording studio, which will help you record voiceover for your courses. Here is the equipment I use for my studio, all of which is portable and inexpensive:

- Blue Yeti Pro USB microphone
- Monoprice 602650 Microphone Isolation Shield
- Audio-Technica ATH-M50x Professional Monitor Headphones
- Auphonix 6-Inch Pop Filter

I've put together a YouTube video to explain how to use the above setup, along with some general recording tips. See YouTube channel Learn Tech Collective.

There are many excellent microphones available on Amazon. Just read the customer reviews. Check the quality of your audio before you do any major projects. Be sure the microphone isn't overloading. Overloaded audio is one of the hardest things to fix. Also, record a little piece of test audio and play it back before you record an entire project. This will help you gauge the quality of your sound and may save you a lot of time fixing audio later.

Here are a few other tips to get you started:

- If you need to travel with your voiceover equipment, keep it in your carry-on luggage whenever possible. I kept the box for my Blue Yeti Pro microphone so I can protect it during travel.
- Carry extra equipment with you when you travel, such as an extra cord for your microphone. Equipment failure happens at the most inconvenient times.
- Always use a pop filter. It really does improve the quality of your voiceover.
- Cover hard surfaces near the microphone with soft blankets, carpet samples, or pillows. Place a blanket on the surface beneath the microphone.
- Try to minimize ambient sound by turning off the air conditioner and any equipment or machinery near you. If

you're sitting in a chair, make sure it doesn't squeak. Be careful not to knock the microphone while recording.

- Make sure your gain is set correctly. Mine is usually set to 10 o'clock, although your setting may very well be different. Also be sure that you are using the cardioid pattern, which is symbolized by an upside-down heart. Your microphone will come with a manual that explains any other settings.

There are lots of variables to consider when recording audio. You may be picking up a buzz from company machinery or an air conditioning unit. If possible, turn off anything that produces sound before you record. (That includes phones!) If you can't turn off equipment, at least make sure that the voice you are recording can be heard clearly so you can edit out the background noise later. Try to avoid picking up echoes. If needed, hang up blankets or curtains to make the room "sound" better. It may look ridiculous, but it helps!

You will likely purchase multiple microphones. Boom microphones and lavaliers are ideal for location shoots. For virtual training, you will want a headset or a stand microphone. Both are easy to plug into a computer and will keep the presenter's hands free.

Using the points described above, determine whether doing in-house video and audio production is practical for your company. If it is not and you definitely want to pursue creating videos, identify at least two or three small firms who can handle your production needs. Get pricing information from these firms and relay to your leadership. If you want to pursue in-house video production, ask leadership for a budget and begin researching what the appropriate equipment will cost. Jot down some notes here about how you want to proceed.

#3 Delivering Exams and Assessments

Your learning management system may have tools to help you deliver exam or assessment content. You can deliver questions in several different formats. These may include multiple-choice, essay, and fill-in-the-blank. A user might also "answer" questions by playing games.

If your LMS doesn't offer exam building tools, you can build them in another program, e.g., Captivate, and import them. You will typically import an exam if it has interactive elements since most learning management systems do not offer exam tools that create interactive content.

If you want to design an exam in another program and import it, ask your LMS vendor what you need to do so the exam can be "graded" by your learning management system. It is important that the exam be able to communicate a student's progress to the LMS so it can be recorded as part of their transcript.

#4

Delivering Surveys

Most learning management systems allow you to build and deliver ungraded exams, i.e., surveys. These can be helpful in a variety of ways! Maybe you can ask employees to give anonymous feedback on their leaders through your LMS? Or use surveys to deliver company paperwork electronically?

How can you use the survey function of your learning management system? If desired, ask others how they use surveys in the LinkedIn group.

#5

Delivering Documents

You will likely deliver all of your electronic documents in PDF form unless your LMS has a built-in "document viewer" software. Be sure computers accessing the LMS have PDF viewing software installed. My favorite is Adobe Reader. You can download it for free:

http://get.adobe.com/reader/

What documents would you like to deliver in an electronic format? Write some ideas below.

#6

Electronic Signatures

Most learning management systems allow a user to open up a document, then "electronically sign" it by checking a box. Electronic signatures are easily tracked, and they are a great alternative to having employees sign physical documents. For example, you can choose to host all of your new hire paperwork through your learning management system.

This is a great process because it eliminates a lot of unnecessary paper and makes it easy to track how many employees have completed specific forms. The downside of this is, in the event of a system outage, you may lose access to employment records temporarily. Before deciding to use electronic signatures in place of physical signatures, please consult your corporate legal counsel.

How can you use the electronic signature function of your LMS? Jot down your ideas.

#7 Mobile Devices

What mobile devices will be used to access your LMS? Phones? Tablets? As you design e-learning content, carefully evaluate whether users will be able to access class materials from various devices. Can activities be performed with either a mouse or a touchscreen? If a user has a smartphone, will their screen size be too small to adequately view content? Many e-learning development applications include responsive design features that help you optimize how courses appear on different devices.

Do you have course materials that need to be optimized for viewing on mobile devices? If so, list the three highest priority projects below. If desired, use the LinkedIn group to ask for advice about converting your materials to a more responsive format. Every project is a little different!

#8 Content Accessibility/Multiple Languages

Entire books have been written on how to make e-learning content friendly to those who have special needs, or a different primary language. These topics are definitely worth researching depending on the needs of your employees.

Here are a few thoughts to get you started:

- Consider delivering content both visually and verbally within your e-learning presentations. In other words, the words shown in the presentation should mirror the words being spoken. You can also provide closed captioning or audio transcripts.
- Make sure your training are friendly to those who are color-blind or have partial sight. Visit Lighthouse International (www.lighthouse.org) for more information.
- Analyze your employee base. Which primary languages are most prevalent? What classes should you offer in multiple languages?

Learn more about accessibility issues through:

www.accesslearning.net

#9 Legal Considerations

Does your company span multiple states or countries? If you are delivering content that is influenced by laws or regulations (such as an employee benefits presentation) you may need to create multiple versions of the same training to accommodate all company locations. Many learning management systems include an “audience targeting” function that will allow you to assign appropriate training by geographic area. Ask your vendor for more information.

Reflect on which of your current training courses may benefit from multiple versions.

When designing training, keep in mind that the wording you use may have legal implications. For example, you may want to avoid using the word “exam” in your materials, because it implies that an employee's status within your company is dictated by their performance on tests. Be sure to speak with your legal department for other considerations around your training content.

#10 Get content from all company departments!

Don't you love delegation? If you are trying to create e-learning content quickly, get all of your company's departments involved in the course creation process.

Many learning professionals feel like they need to buy content in order to "fill up" their LMS. The fact is, you may already have great content lurking on your SharePoint or in your document management system. Ask other departments to look in the following places for training presentations, handouts, and videos:

- Company intranet
- Shared network drives
- Document management system
- Marketing material library
- Other learning management systems (if you have more than one)
- Company YouTube or Vimeo channel
- Any other storage repositories, such as external drives

Have departments give you "raw" training content that you can mold into courses. Even your organization's newsletter may contain information you can use! Making an effort to find such materials will decrease your workload, get departments excited about the LMS, and ensure that all departments are represented equally in your training materials.

5

Maintaining the System & Handling Technical Issues

There's a reason the above topics are rolled into one chapter. If system maintenance is performed regularly, you can prevent the majority of technical issues. Now is the time to anticipate problems and put measures in place to alleviate those issues.

Be sure there are specific procedures laid out for common system tasks. This will ensure that those tasks are completed accurately and to the same standards each time.

PRACTICAL TIPS FOR THE DAILY TASKS

Once your LMS is implemented, continue to think about ways to improve administrative practices. Sometimes the habits we form early in the system's life stay with us, even though we could do things more efficiently. Always ask yourself: Is it best for us to continue using the current procedure? Is there a better way? If there is, put a new procedure in place and communicate it to the administrator group.

#1 Course Creation Guidelines

When you or your administrators create courses, you will enter certain pieces of information into the LMS. This information includes the course title, duration, type of course, e.g., instructor-led or virtual, and links to any content, e.g., videos and documents, that will open as part of the class. (Because every LMS is different, the information you associate with courses will vary.) A "course profile" will be created for any class tracked by the LMS. This includes training that is not completed within the system, such as instructor-led classes.

If multiple administrators are creating courses, your lead administrator should communicate clear guidelines for creating courses. Course profiles should be filled out as completely as possible, and the information entered should be accurate. This will help employees find your course when searching the LMS. Many systems allow users to search for courses by title, subject matter, and more.

You may find it useful to create groupings or "catalogs" within the LMS for courses that are similar. For example, you could create one catalog for all courses delivered in French, another for Spanish, etc. You could also group courses by level, subject matter, and numerous other criteria. You can include a course in several different catalogs. For instance, a course can be cataloged as Spanish, 100-level, and Finance all at once.

As a side note… Depending on your system, a "catalog" may be called something else. You may also have sub-catalogs and curricula.

What is the benefit of using catalogs? First, it provides organization so your administrators can find courses easily when working in the system's administrative area. It also makes it easier to create relationships between courses that can be used to automatically assign courses or track employee progress. Creating catalogs early on will allow you to automatically assign courses to your employees with the least amount of effort.

For instance, you can arrange your Accounting catalog so that when a user completes a 100-level class, they are automatically assigned the 200-level class, and so on. This is commonly known as assigning course prerequisites.

You can also create two courses that are considered equivalent in terms of their credit value. You may have two 100-level Accounting classes, and a learner can complete either class to become eligible for 200-level enrollment. This is commonly referred to as creating equivalencies.

For more information on this topic, check out the video resource available to members of the LinkedIn group.

If you are in the process of implementing your LMS, the vendor may provide an import spreadsheet that will allow you to assign prerequisites and equivalencies in one go. This will save you the manual work of filling in this information after the implementation.

#2 Who should have access to the "password reset" function? (If you intend to enable single sign-on for your LMS, skip this section.)

Sure, the password reset function seems harmless. But from practical experience, this function can wreak more havoc on your system in less time than any other system tool. I'm not naming names here, but I know a company that had 75,000 passwords reset at the same time! It was an accident, of course. An admin was trying to reset ONE password and hit the wrong button. Here's where it gets interesting.

In order for the LMS to automatically reset the passwords, it had to be able to send new passwords to employees by email. The company in question did not provide anyone outside of leadership with email addresses. So, guess what? **All 75,000 passwords** had to be reset, one by one, by the administrator team.

Don't let this happen to you. Be selective about which admin levels have access to your reset password function. This goes for any other sensitive functions within your system. Mistakes will still happen, but they will be less likely and less horrifying!

List who, or what roles, will reset passwords.

#3 Is there a "paper version" of training content you can use when the system is down?

It would be great if every LMS was fully operational one hundred percent of the time. However, for any system, there are outages. Plan ahead! If you need all employees to finish a compliance training by a particular date, make sure you have a paper version of that training available in the event of system downtime. Employees will still be able to complete the training on time, and you can enter the data manually later on. A paper alternative is also useful when you need to complete training quickly, and you don't have enough computers to reach all of your employees.

Look through your existing virtual training and decide if there are any critical enough to require a paper alternative. Write them below. Keep in mind as you are creating new e-learning courses that you may need to create a paper version of them as well. If needed, create a procedure to ensure a paper version if new content is created.

#4

Create a living document (FAQ) that explains common technical issues and solutions.

This document will preserve the sanity of your administrator team like nothing else. Your lead administrator should keep an eye out for common technical issues and questions that the administrator team addresses multiple times per week. A document should be created that addresses these issues. Hang the document next to company computers and place a link to it on the LMS user interface. This will greatly cut down on the administrator team's workload!

Ask the administrator team what LMS technical support questions they get the most. List these questions below. Use them to create an FAQ document using the template available from the LinkedIn group, if desired.

#5 Create a living document that addresses system requirements.

Every learning management system has a list of system requirements. These are elements that the LMS needs in order to run correctly on a user's computer. These requirements may include specific versions of Java, Flash Player, and browsers. You can get a list of requirements from your LMS vendor. Share this list with all LMS administrators and your IT department. Ensure that the list is updated as requirements change.

As a side note, there may also be requirements from the LMS vendor regarding the format of e-learning courses tracked within the system. Some of these rules may be associated with how the course protocols (SCORM, AICC, and Tin Can/xAPI) are set up. Course protocols are introduced in Chapter 4.

Write your system requirements below. If desired, post questions about your system or e-learning course requirements in the LinkedIn group.

TRACKING TRAINING

As far as your LMS is concerned, training takes place in one of two forms. There are trainings that take place outside of the LMS (such as instructor-led classes) and inside of the LMS (such as e-learning modules hosted within the LMS). A learning management system automatically tracks any class completed within the system.

If a learner completes content on their computer but outside of the LMS, it might be trackable using xAPI. (See Chapter 4 for a quick introduction.) If a class takes place outside of the LMS and it isn't tracked by xAPI, the system has no way of knowing what was completed. The instructor or administrator has to enter that information manually.

#1

Training Data Audits

A training data audit should be performed periodically by a high-level administrator, ideally the lead super admin. Training data reports are pulled out of the system and analyzed to ensure data was entered accurately and honestly. On rare occasions, a training data audit will catch a system quirk, such as duplicated data. Harmless, but worth finding so the issue can be fixed by your LMS vendor.

For more information on this topic, check out a corresponding video on YouTube channel Learn Tech Collective.

How many admins enter training data into your LMS? Are those employees judged based on the training data being produced? Let me give an example. If corporate trainers are entering data, and their promotions or salary increases hinge on the number of employees they train, your trainers have a motive to falsify training data. This can be done by double-entering classes, entering classes that were never actually performed, and inflating the number of minutes of training performed in a given class.

If trainers are entering compliance classes that haven't really been completed, you may have a real legal issue. Regardless, your numbers won't be accurate, and it will be difficult to gauge which classes have truly been completed. You may be rolling your eyes and thinking that a trainer wouldn't bother entering extra training just to inflate their numbers, but I've actually seen it happen a number of times, particularly when a promotion or salary increase was on the line. Data can also be entered incorrectly due to human error or a misunderstanding of the data entry process.

You can double-check LMS training data by asking a trainer for written records of their classes, e.g., sign-in sheets, asking leadership if the classes have actually been performed, and asking employees if they did indeed attend the classes that are on their transcripts.

If you have reason to believe the training data in your LMS is inaccurate, speak with the trainer who entered the data and try to determine whether data was intentionally entered incorrectly. Look for patterns in the trainer's data over time. If you believe the trainer purposely falsified records, you may have grounds for disciplinary action, up to and including termination. If you believe the trainer made an innocent mistake, a simple retraining on data entry will likely fix the issue.

Your lead super administrator should establish a procedure for training data audits. This procedure may detail how often audits will be conducted, which parties will be audited, and whether or not audits will be random. (In other words, you could randomly choose a few trainers to audit every period.) Conducting random audits saves time because it limits the number of trainers being checked within a given period.

Write out the procedure for audits.

Manual Sign-in Sheets

#2

Employees who attend instructor-led training are often asked to place their name on a sign-in sheet so their attendance can be recorded. If your company does not provide a sign-in sheet template for trainers to use, it is helpful to create one. Include columns for the employees' printed names, ID numbers (if applicable), and their signatures. At the top of the sheet, include space for the trainer to write in the course that is being completed, along with the LMS course ID, and the current date.

If desired, download the manual sign-in sheet template available to members of Learn Tech Collective.

Once an instructor-led class is completed, the information on the sign-in sheet will be entered manually into the LMS for tracking purposes. This is why creating a sign-in sheet template is important. Using a template ensures that the person entering the class data later has the information they need.

It is important for data to be entered into the system in a timely manner so that data reports are always accurate. In the case of compliance courses, it is also important for the date of course completion to be accurate. Here's an example as to why.

Let's say an employee is terminated for inappropriate sexual behavior in the workplace. The employee attempts to sue your company, saying that sexual harassment training was not provided during her employment, and she did not know her behavior was inappropriate. If you are able to show the employee was given harassment training before the date of her inappropriate behavior, you may be able to prevent the lawsuit. This is one reason to ensure your training data is accurate.

Consider whether you want to have trainers keep written records, such as sign-in sheets, for a set period of time. This may assist you in conducting training data audits, as discussed in **tip #1**. If you decide to have your trainers retain such records, communicate this to the appropriate employees immediately.

#3 Electronic Sign-in Sheets

There is an alternative to maintaining manual sign-in sheets for LMS data entry purposes. You can instead create an electronic sign-in sheet that trainers can download onto their computers. This electronic sheet collects the same information as a manual sheet (listed in **tip #2**). You can create an electronic sign-in sheet in Excel and send it to all trainers. As employees enter the classroom, they will stop by the trainer's computer and enter their information into the sheet.

This procedure allows information to be collected in typed form, which is great if some of your employees write in hieroglyphics. Depending on your learning management system, you may be able to import an Excel spreadsheet directly into the system, which eliminates the need for manual data entry. Ask your LMS vendor if this is a possibility. The format of such a spreadsheet will vary by vendor.

Before you begin using electronic sign-in sheets, speak with your legal department to be sure you do not need to have physical signatures from employees who are attending certain classes. You may need to implement a separate signature form for instructor-led compliance courses, such as sexual harassment training.

SYSTEM OUTAGES

System outages, both expected and unexpected, are going to happen. Your LMS vendor will schedule downtime that is required to maintain the system. Scheduled downtime will typically occur at off-hours and should not affect your business unless your company spans multiple time zones. However, as with any system, there will be unexpected failures. Anticipate these issues and have a strategy prepared.

#1 When the system is down, how quickly will you need it back up?

What is the priority? Set a benchmark so you know how the administrator team should approach a system outage.

If you haven't already, review the Service Level Agreement (SLA) within your vendor agreement. An SLA outlines how, and how quickly, the vendor will respond to system failures and outages. If you are selecting an LMS, this is something to discuss with your vendor. If you already have an LMS, it's a good idea to look up your SLA, so you know what type of response to expect if the system fails.

See YouTube channel Learn Tech Collective for advice on negotiating an SLA.

#2 What support is available to you if you experience an urgent technical issue?

The time to explore this issue is now before the LMS is down and you have executives poking you for answers. Does your LMS vendor have set hours? Any availability on the weekend? Let's say your company spans multiple time zones. If your vendor only offers support from nine to five EST, how will this affect your ability to respond to unexpected outages?

Is your super administrator team exempt or non-exempt? Does your lead administrator have the ability to access the learning management system from home? (You may need to provide a laptop with a company VPN if your system is based on your company's intranet.) If you have expectations that your admin team will be on-call to provide emergency support, have you communicated this? Do you need to create a schedule for the admin team, detailing which days each admin will be on call for off-hours emergencies?

List the possible sources of support in the event of a system outage. Note if these sources are available during off-hours.

HELPING EMPLOYEES EMBRACE THE LMS

It is always a challenge to get an entire employee base to embrace new technology. However, you have an advantage, because your LMS will definitely benefit your employees. It's just a matter of communicating this fact to them in such a way that they accept and embrace the system. Getting started early makes things that much easier.

#1 Help tech-challenged employees adjust to computer-based learning.

Depending on the nature of your company, you may have a lot of employees who are not computer-savvy. If this is the case, you will want to begin doing remedial computer training with employees as soon as possible. You may need to start with absolute basics, such as how to use a mouse and keyboard, and basic functions such as how to open the Windows Start menu. Consider creating videos that go over this content, or use existing tutorials from the Internet. You might also invest in a classroom training from a local Windows provider. If you are unsure of your employees' levels of comfort with computers, you may want to send out a survey or discuss the matter with direct supervisors to determine where you need to start.

If you will offer introductory computer classes, write the nature of these classes below. If desired, ask for advice in the LinkedIn group.

#2 Make it clear that the LMS is not going away.

Every company has its fair share of "techn-ostriches," people who bury their head in the sand when technology comes along and hope it will go away before they have to learn it. Make sure employees understand that the learning management system is not a company experiment. It is here to stay! That way, your employees will invest the time and effort to learn how to use it. This may be slow-going at first, but the more enthusiastic you can be in promoting your LMS, the faster it will go.

6

Realizing the Value of Your LMS

Running a successful learning management system is not enough! You want to utilize the system efficiently and communicate the value of your LMS to all of the stakeholders in your company. This chapter offers some suggestions on how to utilize your LMS to its fullest.

Use the Features of the LMS to Your Advantage

The more administrator tasks you can automate, the more your admin team will thank you. This section revisits ways you can utilize your LMS efficiently.

#1 Use Excel to sort data reports and provide performance insights.

Learning management systems offer many options in terms of reporting training data that has been recorded. Your LMS will likely offer the three reports described below at the very least, and most systems offer quite a bit more.

- A transcript of all courses completed by a particular user.
    - Includes the employee's name, ID, courses completed with corresponding dates, and any grades associated with courses.
- A "completed courses" report that shows all employees who have finished a course or group of courses you specify.
    - If your company is performing a training initiative, or you want to see data for a specific compliance course, this is the perfect report to analyze.
- An "incomplete courses" report is basically the opposite of the completed courses report. It tells you which users have not yet completed a course or courses.
    - Let's say you are using your LMS to deliver a particular course on harassment. You have decided

to make this course mandatory for employees to complete every two years of employment. You can create an incomplete course report that automatically runs that course's history for the past two years, showing who in your company has not yet completed the course within the given timeframe. This makes it easier for you to keep employees on track.

Many LMS reports are delivered in the form of an Excel document, specifically a CSV. LMS data reports are often not stylish. They are plain tables of data with no formatting. (Some learning management systems offer additional reporting tools that create beautiful tables and graphics.) The great part about CSV files is that they are easily sortable in Excel. You can, therefore, transform plain data reports into useful scorecards for your training team or executive leadership. If you need an explanation of how to sort by column, delete rows, or total data, there are excellent tutorials available from Microsoft.com.

#2 Create automatic/recurring reports to track the progress of training initiatives.

In addition to running a data report on a one-time basis, many learning management systems allow you to set a report to recur automatically and send results to one user or multiple users. For example, let's say you have a training initiative that you want to track on a weekly basis. You can have the learning management system generate an updated copy of a particular report each week, on a day that you specify. Frequently you don't even have to log onto the LMS to access a copy of this report. You can simply have a copy of the report sent to your email address. This can save you time depending on how many initiatives you're tracking. Ask your LMS vendor to explain the entire reporting section of your system so you can benefit from any time-saving tools.

#3 Set assessments to automatically reassign until employees achieve a certain level of competency.

One of the major advantages of any learning management system is the ability to assign assessments to employees. These assessments can come at the end of a course, or they can stand alone. You can also set a required pass grade. This means that if you want employees to achieve at least 80% on an exam, you can tell the LMS to reassign the exam until the employee achieves 80% or higher. There are numerous settings that you can apply to an exam to dictate how it behaves when it is reassigned. For example, you can have the exam automatically scramble the questions so that the employee does not see them in their original order. You can also set up an exam question bank so that the exam will generate a slightly different set of questions every time it is opened.

#4 Assemble a "college catalog" of increasingly challenging courses.

As discussed previously, you can automatically assign courses to employees based on previous course completion. For instance, let's say you have a series of classes on Retail Management. You can have courses that are at the basic level, or 100 level, as well as more advanced courses - 200 level, 300 level, and so on. Once an employee completes the 100 level course, you can have the LMS automatically assign 200 level courses, so employees always have another set of courses to complete. This type of automatic assignment is typically easy to do. Ask your LMS vendor for instructions.

Here is an activity to help you assess the structure of your training program. (A corresponding template is available in your LinkedIn group materials!) Develop a list of all classes you have available in your company. Categorize classes as e-learning, virtual, or instructor-led. Also categorize by subject matter, such as Finance.

Then organize classes by level. For instance, you may have a basic class about margin that falls under the Finance heading, and a more advanced margin class that builds on the content in the first class. Once you assemble classes in order of difficulty, you should be able to determine the order in which classes should be completed. From there, it is easy to decide how you want to set up the auto-assignment features in your LMS.

Hint: To complete this activity, you may want to write out all course titles on different Post-It notes that are color-coded by subject matter. This will allow you to move your course titles around until you have them assembled in a sensible order.

#5 Ensure compliance courses, such as harassment training, are automatically assigned and completed on time.

Learning management systems can automatically assign and reassign courses as needed. This is particularly useful for legal and compliance courses because you can have the system auto-assign classes based on a timetable you set. For instance, if you have a recertification training that must be completed every two years, you can easily set up the assignment to recur automatically every two years.

Below, write down compliance courses and other classes that must be completed multiple times within an employee's employment history. Use this list to decide which courses you are going to automatically assign.

#6 Assign monthly safety courses with the intention of decreasing Workers Comp.

Is your company having issues with a specific type of Workers Compensation claims, such as back injuries or lacerations? If so, you may want to assign classes aimed at reducing those types of claims. For instance, you could address back injury claims by creating classes on ergonomics and proper lifting techniques. The classes you create don't have to be fancy. They may just consist of a fun, informative document or short video.

An important part of safety training is consistency. Create a series of twelve safety topics that will be assigned, one by one, at the beginning of every month. This could be the beginning of your safety training program if you do not already have one. You can set each topic to be auto-assigned to the entire employee base months in advance so that you don't have to worry about it.

Ask your HR department for information on your company's Workers Compensation claims. Is there a claim type that is particularly prevalent? What kind of training might help your company decrease the number of claims? Write down some safety topics that are of interest to your organization. If desired, ask other members of the LinkedIn group for ideas.

#7 Make it easier for employees to find and register for upcoming instructor-led classes.

Learning management systems are good for more than just assigning e-learning classes. They are also excellent at managing and promoting instructor-led classes. You can often advertise upcoming classes on the LMS home page, and employees can register in a couple of steps. The procedure to create class sessions and register for classes will vary depending on your system. Ask your LMS vendor for instructions.

If you are concerned about employees signing up for classes and forgetting to inform their supervisor, you can require that a class be approved by a supervisor before the employee is formally registered. Again, check with your vendor for details.

Jot down some ways to motivate more employees to register for classes in the LMS. If desired, ask the Learn Tech Collective's LinkedIn group for advice.

#8 Easily coordinate classes that involve students from multiple locations by reserving seats for each location.

Through your LMS, there are a lot of ways to make scheduling instructor-led classes more efficient. Available tools vary by system, but many learning management systems help you coordinate classes involving employees from multiple locations. You simply tell the LMS how many total seats you will make available for a given session, then tell the system how many seats to reserve for each location in attendance.

For example, let's say you reserve five seats for employees from your Southern location. An employee from your Northern location would not be able to register for one of these seats, even if it was the only spot left. If all five seats are already taken by Southern employees, the sixth Southern employee who tries to register will receive a notification telling them that the class is booked. He or she can choose to be placed on the session's reserve list. If another Southern employee withdraws from the class, a seat will be automatically assigned to the employee on the reserve list. The employee may also receive a notification email depending on the settings you have enabled in your LMS. These are all good subjects to discuss with your LMS vendor.

#9 Use LMS registration to accurately predict how many students will attend training. Quickly track employee attendance following class sessions and report to supervisors.

Having employees register for classes through the LMS makes it easy for administrators to track attendees. It is easy for instructors to see who has signed up for a session, and print out a roster of those they are expecting.

Obviously, the roster is not always going to be accurate. From practical experience, you can expect that fifteen percent of registrants will either drop the class after registering or simply not show up. However, an estimated headcount is helpful when budgeting for catering, room rentals, and other classroom elements. If a registered employee doesn't make a class, you can communicate with their supervisor.

Here is one way you can use a list of class registrants. If your LMS offers a course roster, print it out, so you have a list of everyone who is expected to attend. As employees arrive, have them initial next to their name on your course roster. That way, you can easily see if any employees are absent. Printed course rosters can be used in place of the manual sign-in sheets.

MOTIVATE AN INCREASE IN TRAINING

Increasing the amount of employee training is good for everyone involved. Supervisors get more out of their employees, employees move up in the company faster, and the entire corporate structure benefits! Here are some ways you can motivate supervisors and employees to participate in more training.

#1 Determine what "training success" looks like in relation to your LMS. Set a benchmark.

As discussed at the beginning of this book, it is important to define what goals your executive leadership has for your system. Based on their goals, you should be able to draw a picture of what a successful learning management system looks like. Use this picture to put together some specific goals for your LMS.

Here are some goal examples.

- Convert and deliver all compliance courses through an electronic format for more accurate records.
- Increase safety awareness and decrease workplace injuries by implementing a year-round series of safety courses.
- Upload most employment documents to the LMS to make their delivery more efficient.
- Create a specific number of courses targeted at each level of leadership.

- Develop more department-specific training.
- Offer mobile-friendly courses for employees who travel frequently.
- Achieve a particular amount of training per employee.
- Motivate employees to look for and complete courses on their own by using gamification and social learning initiatives.

Discuss what LMS success looks like with executive leadership, and write down the common themes.

#2 Incorporate transcripts into job evaluations and promotion decisions.

Encourage employees to print their course transcripts and provide them to supervisors as part of their job performance reviews. A supervisor may reference an employee's transcript when evaluating promotability, deciding on salary increases, and the like. Incorporating transcripts into job performance reviews reinforces the importance of training in your company culture.

Discuss incorporating transcripts into job performance reviews with HR and other members of leadership. Are they open to the idea? What challenges will you face in getting them to embrace the concept?

#3 Set a target amount of training time per employee.

It is important to set a benchmark of how much training time each employee should receive within a given time frame. In order to set this benchmark, you may want to study the training data collected during the first quarter your LMS is fully functional. Use this data to get an idea of how much training time employees are currently receiving, and how much of an increase may be realistic.

It's easy to get a rough idea of the average time each employee spends on training. Pull a data report that includes all training performed by all employees during a specified period. (Your LMS vendor can provide instructions.) Total all of the training durations that appear within the report, then divide the total time by how many employees you currently have in your company. This will give you an idea of how much training the average employee received during your specified time frame.

Based on this estimated average, you can decide how much of an increase in training you would like to see. Setting a benchmark will help you motivate executive leadership, supervisors, employees, and others to work toward a stronger training culture. You can also include the average amount of training received by each employee on company recruiting materials. *("Look how much career development you will get by working at Acme, Inc.!")*

As a side note, setting a target amount of training doesn't tell you whether the training was valuable to the employee, or even retained. It's always a good idea to follow up with learners a few days after they've learned something new to see if they remember what they learned and if they have questions.

If you are teaching a complex topic, try to teach it in bite-sized chunks (short videos are great for this!) and have learners complete related activities in between the lessons. You can try this during your LMS rollout. Send a daily email to your new LMS administrators and include a short video and task to complete in the new LMS. Have each administrator send a screenshot or answer a question related to the task you asked them to complete. Enter each person who responds into a drawing for a gift card.

What is your target amount of training time per employee? How long do you believe it will take to achieve this target amount? Other than training time, what are some other methods you can use to determine whether employees are retaining and applying what they are learning? If desired, discuss with other members of the LinkedIn group.

#4 Create an automatically-assigned curriculum for new employees so they can start learning immediately.

As discussed earlier in this section, you can group courses by subject matter and catalog them by level. Once you have done this, it is easy to assign groups of related classes to employees based on their hire date, department, and other employment factors. Create a group of classes specifically for new hires and have the system auto-assign it to employees. This curriculum could include all electronic documents associated with new hire paperwork, some basic classes on safety and harassment, and any other classes you consider to be important for a new employee, such as classes on company culture and leadership. You can also include courses to be auto-assigned after a week or 30 days, so the new hire continues to build their knowledge. Auto-assignment saves your administrators time and ensures employees have instant access to classes appropriate to their level.

Determine what classes should be assigned to a new hire. Decide if there are any additional classes you need to create specifically for this level. Make notes below. If desired, ask what others assign to new hires by using the LinkedIn group.

#5

Create a list of electives that employees can take when there is downtime. Provide incentives, so employees are motivated to complete the electives.

Once you have a healthy number of classes available within your LMS, you might consider creating educational games and activities that employees can work on when they have downtime. Classes could be on a variety of topics, such as company culture, notable members of leadership, product knowledge, and customer service.

If e-learning classes are made available to employees when things are slow, you will hopefully be able to utilize that time in a positive fashion. You can motivate employees by offering small prizes - gift cards or extra vacation time - and sponsoring competitions between teams.

Speak with your leadership and determine some appropriate elective topics. Also, discuss how you are going to reward employees for completing extra training. A little gift certificate goes a long way! Jot your ideas below and share with others in the LinkedIn group.

#6 Create "how-to" videos for common technical questions. Point employees to that content when they need technical assistance.

Consider offering technical support e-learning classes through your LMS! For instance, if your IT department gets a lot of questions about setting up an Outlook account, you may want to create an instructional video on the subject and post it on your LMS. Your IT department can direct employees to the videos when they have technical issues, thereby saving your IT department valuable labor time.

Ask your IT department what questions they commonly get from employees requesting technical support. Determine whether any of these common topics would benefit from a training video or interactive course. If so, list those topics below.

Communicating the Success of Your LMS

By now, you have done a tremendous amount of work to ensure the success of your LMS. Congratulations! Remember to communicate your system's progress to those in leadership as well as your learners. Below are some ways you can continue to promote your learning management system within your company.

#1 Link promotability to completion of certain courses.

Encourage employees to complete more classes by linking training to promotability. For instance, you can require that a person moving into a supervisor role complete at least two finance courses, three leadership courses, and so on. Creating a course catalog of these courses could come in handy, as it would be an easy reference to employees looking to move up in the company.

If you choose to make course completion part of the criteria for promotions, you'll want to add this information to appropriate job descriptions. You will also want to communicate this information clearly to all of your employees, so they are aware of the change.

Speak with leadership regarding the feasibility of adding training completion to the requirements for promotions. You may want to look at existing job descriptions before discussing this possibility with leadership, as there may already be some training requirements listed.

#2 Create competition by releasing training statistics by team.

We've talked about the benefits of competition, but it's worth discussing again. Increasing the amount of training your employees complete is easy. Just create competition between departments and locations! One way to do this is to run LMS reports showing how much training time is being completed by each of your departments or locations. (If your LMS offers gamification features, be sure to utilize them.) Collate this data, total it, and release it in a pretty scorecard to all of your departments. Offer a prize for the department that completes the most training. Congratulate top-performing departments in front of your executive leadership. Supervisors in other departments will likely devote more resources to training in coming periods.

#3 Deliver training data summaries to leadership by creating simple, easy-to-read scorecards.

The training reports available from your LMS are useful not only to administrators, but also to keep executive leadership apprised of what is going on with your training program. As we have discussed, you can easily run data reports that show how much training time has been completed by employees over a specified period. This information can be used to create training scorecards that show a summary of important metrics. You can be as general or specific as you like within your training scorecard, but it is best to keep an executive summary of data to two pages or less. If there are particular legal or compliance courses that executive leadership is interested in, this would be a great time to show off statistics pertaining to those training. Depending on your company, you may want to release such a scorecard to your executive leadership every fiscal period, quarter, or bi-annually.

#4 Continue communicating training opportunities to the learner.

Be deliberate and consistent in your communications to the learner population. Remind them of the training opportunities available to them, and involve them in your marketing efforts.

Here are some ways to communicate with your learners:

- Create an employee advisory committee to preview content, give feedback, and advise on what new content should be developed. Ask the committee to assist in promoting your training initiatives through word of mouth.
- Attend organizational meetings and give a short update on new training content and upcoming classes.
- Use gamification and social learning initiatives to stimulate an interest in learning.

- Create a branding scheme, and then advertise content and initiatives in multiple mediums. You can create branded posters, desktop wallpapers, emails, and the like.
- Release training information on a regular and consistent basis. You can establish a monthly email newsletter for example, with links to register for classes and access content within the LMS.
- Target your communications, so they are relevant to the recipient. You may need to create multiple training newsletters for various departments so you can ensure the content is relevant to them.

Check out YouTube channel Learn Tech Collective for more ideas, and post in the LinkedIn group if you would like to share your thoughts.

#5

Remember to compare the past to the present. Your new learning management system has hopefully made life easier for you and a number of other people in your organization. Make sure you give leadership an accurate picture of the before and after. Here are some items to think about:

- How long did it used to take a learner to search for an e-learning course or register for an instructor-led course? How much time does it take when using the new LMS? How much is that time worth?

- How long did you used to spend compiling the data you needed for compliance purposes? How much time are you saving with the new LMS?

- Think of any tasks that were significantly shortened or made easier for the learners or LMS administrators. Determine how long those tasks would have taken in the past, and assign a monetary value to the time you are now saving.

This is the last activity! It's your turn now. What clever tips and tricks do you have for learning management system administration? Post your ideas and feedback to the LinkedIn group.

THAT'S ALL, FOLKS!

THANK YOU FOR READING!

IF YOU LEARNED SOMETHING FROM THIS BOOK, PLEASE HELP OTHERS FIND IT BY RATING IT ON AMAZON.COM OR DISCUSSING IT ON OUR SOCIAL MEDIA PAGES.

www.facebook.com/rofl411

www.twitter.com/rofl411

www.youtube.com/learntechcollective

HOPE TO HEAR FROM YOU SOON!

- KAT

Supporters

My most sincere thanks to the following individuals who contributed a combined total of $4,883 to support the republishing of this book, along with *The LMS Selection Checklist.* I appreciate your support of my work, and I hope you enjoy the finished product!

Sandra Cutler

Kevin Gumienny

Gene Idol

Adib Masumian

Heather Poggi-Mannis

Kent Russell

Matthew Sime

Renee Sopeta

Donald Twining

Karin Zijlstra

...and a few anonymous donors

About the Author

Katrina Marie Baker owns Resources of Fun Learning, a learning and development publishing and consulting firm. Her clients range from Fortune 100 companies to small businesses. Katrina has also worked in global training capacities for a Fortune 500 retailer and two of the world's most prestigious law firms. In addition to this book, Katrina has authored *The LMS Selection Checklist* and *Corporate Training Tips & Tricks*.

Katrina is a former Director of Technology with the Association for Talent Development, and she speaks at national and international events on LMS and e-learning topics. She has implemented over 25 learning management systems and mentored top-tier executives in the aerospace, legal, retail, and technology industries.

www.linkedin.com/in/katrinabaker

13698474R00100

Printed in Great Britain
by Amazon